It was about a year ago that I read the first half
tional. It was the first book that gave me a close in
intimate issues, such as marriage, loss, success, s̶ .... I have read
many books by women about their bonds of friendship with other women, but very few
give a window into the world of men. I think this book would be unique and invaluable
for both men and women.

The other aspect of the book that made it special was the tension and gripping nature
of the individual stories of these men. It made it very compelling to read, rather than dull
or preachy in the way that self-help books often are. I left off completely engrossed in the
story of the child with the eye disease and couldn't wait to find out how this turned out.

I think this book with its very realistic and warm storyline, fills a profound need in
our society to learn about how to solve everyday problems through the support and caring
of friends. It shows people - better than any self-help book could - the actual words and
approaches that real men use in an actual context. You suggested that I briefly describe
myself so the publishers could get a feel of who was writing this letter. I hold a doctorate
in public health, and have spent 10 years in the UC Berkeley School of Public Health
working on programs to help empower people to become healthier by dealing with everyday
problems. I currently publish the Wellness Guide which has over 1.6 million copies sold.

I hope your prospective publisher will seriously consider the large market for this
wonderful book. I also think that your publisher should consider the potential for movie
rights - this one would be a hit! A couple of titles that occur to me are "Man to Man"
or "In the Company of Men."

Thank you and Good Luck! I am looking forward to seeing this in print.

~ WRITTEN IN 1984 BY LINDA NEUHAUSER D.PH.

Before reading your book, I viewed the Holy Spirit as the utility infielder on a team where
The Father and Son were the stars. Your book has changed my views and rested an old
man's soul: they're separate but equal in the sense that God the Father is to be adored
for the creation and perfection of the Universe, no random event; Jesus is to be loved and
thanked beyond words for saving us from our sinful nature and giving us eternal life (I
still struggle with this on an intellectual basis but try to accept it based on faith. Reading
the Case for Christ and The Case of Faith have helped); and the Holy Spirit who Jesus
gave to us when He ascended to the Father. In a sense the Holy Spirit is a main personage
of the Triune God in that he abides in us. Thanks for that!

I agree that we need to "let go and let God." He created us to be proactive to Do

What Jesus Would Do!! He gave us a free will and wants us to exercise that free will while giving up control knowing that he is there to grieve with us, laugh with us, celebrate with us, and pick us up. The Bible tells us that he prays for us even when we are "prayerless."

An excellent read; worthy of publication; probably one of a kind. Good resource for small groups. Go for it!!!!!!!!!!!!!!

~ART FABSITS

Shirley and I both enjoyed reading your manuscript. Of special interest to Shirley were the principals involved and your follow up of their individual problems. Although their problems remained, they individually created their own solutions. I, Shirley, understand the text as meaning that the Holy Spirit in our own hearts can and will make us a happier and loving person.

I too am in accord with Shirley's thoughts and if one thing remains in my mind was your Chapter 7, especially your review of the biblical text of I Corinthians and how it applies to all. All my life I have never had a good explanation of my relationship to God. Again your Chapter 7 is my total explanation and understanding of God and the Holy Spirit.

They say that if writing conveys a single thought it is considered a success, therefore, we believe your writing will be a success.

With Love and "DWJWD"

~HENRY AND SHIRLEY RANKIN

Your book touches a deep level with me. At the end my body was warm, my brain (the rational side of me) was in quiet remission and a couple tears slipped from my eyes onto my cheeks. Really thoughtful and feeling centered book...

For me the strong parts of the book were around the emotional sufferings and joys that the men experienced. The emotional dimension of the stories and the book itself touched me most. This is the case partly because I have been mostly a rational, head oriented person most of my life. It has been in just the last decade or two that my capacity to feel and express my emotions has opened that side of me in more depth...

Overall, I commend you on the depth of the stories of these six men you have shared with the reader.

I read the book with only a stop for dinner.

~TIM CHRISTOFFERSEN

IN THE COMPANY OF MEN

* Cover photo is the actual location where the story took place

Brian Donohue
with Kathy Mendonca

www.companyofmen.net

ELM HILL

A Division of
HarperCollins Christian Publishing

www.elmhillbooks.com

In the Company of Men

Published in Nashville, Tennessee, by Elm Hill, an imprint of Thomas Nelson. Elm Hill and Thomas Nelson are registered trademarks of HarperCollins Christian Publishing, Inc.

Elm Hill titles may be purchased in bulk for educational, business, fund-raising, or sales promotional use. For information, please e-mail SpecialMarkets@ ThomasNelson.com.

Library of Congress Cataloging-in-Publication Data

Library of Congress Control Number: 2019909411

ISBN 978-1-400325818 (Paperback)
ISBN 978-1-400325825 (eBook)

DEDICATION

This book is dedicated to 4 very special people: my wife Dellyn, "my stars":
Jim and Loretta Starr and "Spock" Kathy Mendonca.

Dellyn is the "Mema" to our 15 grandkids, the "brains" of our family spread
over 4 states across the country and for me, my forever "Dearest"

Jim and Loretta are the cutest seniors you'd ever imagine: he with his full gray
beard hobbling behind and pushing Loretta's wheel chair - just as fragile as frag-
ile can be - but inside roars a bonfire of faith and understanding of the great
sage atop the mountain where pilgrims come from miles away for just a few of
his key words – (we get Jim's wisdom every week at Saturday Morning Men)—
and Loretta, a graduate of Yale Divinity School – both have helped guide the
author's steps on the journey of this story.

Kathy Mendonca, "Spock" to me, took ownership of this story over 5 years ago.
She is as talented as her Star Trek namesake. Her wonderful balance between
a loving heart and mind and the skills of an accomplished teacher, instructional
designer and disciplinarian, has created a work of enormous import
and purpose."

THANK YOU

The Saturday Morning Men (and others) who helped:

Especially Jim Starr and Loretta Starr, Arthur Fabsits, Tim Christofferson, Grayson Grove, Rob Pattison, George Vogt, Ryan Parsons, Marty Koll, Tom Fitterer, Sam Dutcher, Greg Geyer, Jim Mc Clelland, Steve Schmedinghoff, Gerry Long, Bob Fairbanks, Scott Etzel, Michael Penny, Johnny Batista, John Ismen, Greg Reimers, Keith Schroers, Michael Schwan, Joel Isaac, Kevin Murphy, Bob and Terry Johnston, Jenny Hammond, Kat Erbaugh, TJ Burke, Janet Selby, Marisa Barley, Jim Vandersloot, Tristan Brown, Sean Patrick Donohue ("Han Solo") and especially and above all, Kathy Mendonca ("Spock")

The actual six men who shared their lives will remain anonymous!

TABLE OF CONTENTS

Introduction to the Story

This is the true story of six men and how they cope with the crises in their lives:

1. loss of a job/business,
2. relationships with their churches and service clubs,
3. loss of control,
4. life-threatening sickness,
5. incapacitating illness of a son,
6. death of a spouse and increasing age, and ultimately,
7. their understanding and belief in God, Jesus, and the Holy Spirit.

Because it is true, it is replete with failures and heartaches, abuses of power and money, and even emotional illness by persons in positions of responsibility and authority. It shows how men have a unique way of communicating about intimate and personal tragedies, and how they deal with loss. It shows how each individual tries to understand his own values and beliefs, particularly when tested in the harsh realities of today's world. Names and places have been changed as needed.

This book presents an easier and clearer way of thinking about the Holy Spirit and how the Spirit can be active, alive, and exuberant even in a world that seems out of control.

Lastly, it presents an easy to understand image of the Holy Spirit as the common unifying theme that can unite all peoples of the world in a shared vision of God and Jesus.

I hope this makes sense to you.
the Author

CHAPTER 1

STARTING POINT –

AN INTRODUCTION TO THE SIX MEN

This is a true story about six men:

- a high school counselor,
- an electronics guy,
- a retired salesman,
- a pastor,
- a lawyer, and
- an international banker.

It all started one morning over 20 years ago.

the High School Counselor

It was about 6:30 a.m. and the 35 year old high school counselor, who was just plain a "night-person," was trying to wake up in an "orderly fashion," which was not within his personal skills inventory.

So about 15 minutes later, on that particular morning, his wife shook him from his bear-like sleep and said "O.K. sweetie, get out of bed, you're going to be late!" He looked up like the groundhog in Pennsylvania; looked around for one second, and collapsed back into his warm lair.

Coherence began to come slowly into focus, and he thought for a moment about his life, and if whether on this particular Tuesday morning he should get out of bed. He realized again that his wife usually made good sense, though he would rarely admit it. Anyway, the fuzziness seemed to further dissipate and he had to face the fact about what was becoming at this point quite evident: "I'm awake anyway."

His mind flashed that it wasn't so long ago, when his bed was really his hideout, his refuge, his fortress. He had lost 25 pounds, his self-confidence, and his sense of humor (which was always his hallmark). They were all gone, and he stayed in bed because that was the only place where people couldn't see him in his weakened and disabled state. O.K. I'll get up at this ridiculous hour to see the "Bible Boys" down at the coffee shop, because you know, he thought to himself, "I need it."

Eighteen months earlier, this High School Counselor was also quite a different person. He had prayed, and thought, and believed for many years that he would become a Professor of Theology. He had been pursuing his academic work part-time for his Ph.D. in Theology very seriously. He had decided to work with students, to write, lecture, and be their friend. At the same time, he worked at a nearby Christian high school. He had been married for 10 years and thought his life and career were on track. God was good.

Then something unexpected happened: the newly arrived Principal at the High School told him, "*You're really not cut out for work with young people! You had better make some changes in your career plans. You obviously need a new "calling," a new purpose for your life."*

The remarkable thing was that the High School Counselor really loved working with these young high schoolers. He couldn't get over how much he really loved them. He loved being around them, playing games with them, cracking jokes with them, and talking about Jesus with them. He loved it more than what he was doing for his Ph.D. So what should he do about the new Principal telling him that he was *"not cut out to work with young people"?* His heart was telling him something totally different.

What followed was the 25-pound weight loss; the self-doubts, timidity and quietness that he couldn't show to the outside world. While at home, the pain, the anguish and even the embarrassment about his career, his "calling," his life's purpose, were all called into question by this 35 year old, an unforgiving judge, jury, and executioner!

The High School Counselor had also really loved the people that worked with him at Harvest Christian High. He thought about Kate. Kate ran the Community Center at Harvest. She was great fun. She loved the older people who volunteered at the school and community center, the students and everyone in between. She had become the High School Counselor's close friend and over her past eight years at Harvest Christian had won a place in the hearts of many, many people there. Yet, the newly arrived Principal told her that she needed more education and was *"not really cut out for her job with the younger children."*

The new Principal's vision was to grow a high school to double or triple the size of Harvest, as the Principal had supposedly done at his previous assignments. Who was the High School Counselor to question the dreams and aspirations of this new Principal? After all, he was the Principal and thus deserved the total and complete support of the high school staff. After all, the members of the Board of Directors prayed hard and worked hard to find this Principal and the Principal deserved the full trust, love, obedience and devotion of all. Right?

The young High School Counselor remembered asking himself about what must be going on in the Principal's mind. If the Principal was a man of God, then he must be guided by his closeness to Jesus. He must be a man of insight and holiness. He must be the shepherd and I am to be lead, isn't that right? This is what the Bible said. I need to obey! Right?

But his heart was telling him something totally different. He loved working with the junior high and high school kids. He loved their need to be recognized, to be treated as other than a child, to be given authority for what they could handle. He loved to counsel them on their problems, which were vast and serious. He loved dealing with the changes in their hormones and the drama of their first relationships. He loved it. *"God knows I love it!"* How could he feel so lost listening to the advice of his new Principal? Nothing seemed to make sense. Was he that confused about what God wanted of him?

Anyway, he said to himself that *"Yes, I will make it to the "Bible Boys"* this morning, thinking that it was going to be a meeting like all the others.

the Lawyer

"It can't be 3:13 in the morning" he thought. This body of mine seems to be fighting me. What was happening? His body was like an old friend who had turned against him. Cold feet, he couldn't get over his cold feet. He would "ice-up," particularly when sitting at his computer. The thermostat read 70, but his feet were cold, very cold. He had

run a marathon, was known for his boundless energy, but on this morning, this 48 year old lawyer was exhausted just trying to get out of bed.

His mind went over it again. Like so many times before. How did it all happen? Who was to blame? Was anyone to blame? How did God fit into it all? Did God have a hand in his apparent failure? Was this the hand of God at work? Was it all random chance? Did he blow it somehow? Was it all his fault?

How could that be? He had won. He had just beaten four lawyers from one of the largest law firms in the Silicon Valley. But he hadn't made a penny for his family. It was the dream case of his 17-year career: a multi-million-dollar software copyright case in federal court. Then there was the second case: a contract case regarding a chemical patent. He, and his client, had discovered that a chemical in the formulation shipped from Australia contained a cancer-producing agent. He was moving in for the "kill," when the other side went insolvent and deprived him and his family of a six-figure fee. How it hurt! He couldn't understand how it happened. It was so unfair.

Money problems were not the only worry. That past November his mother had died after a sudden heart attack. She had a wonderful life: raising seven children, was a great friend to his father, and had died peacefully in his father's arms. But it was not his mother's death that tore at his soul at all hours of the night. His heart was missing his family back east. When he received the call, he dropped everything to fly home. His wife and children could not come due to the expense and the short notice. When he arrived, a deep sadness engulfed him. He felt the freezing pain of missing his extended family. All three brothers, three sisters and spouses, 16 grandchildren and about 100 relatives and another 100 neighborhood friends were all there for the funeral. Oh the pain of missing this beautiful family was engulfing and overwhelming. It was like a tidal wave of emotions where he could hardly breathe.

Upon his return to northern California, he was in a free fall of homesickness and loneliness. His wife was from the East Coast, and she was ready to move back "in a heartbeat." Their children were all in California: at schools, colleges and working. The thought of moving 3,000 miles away caused a short circuit in his thought process. Memories of growing up with his cousins consumed him. Thinking about how he ended up living on the West Coast, all seemed to be a puzzle from which there was no solution. Yet the questions came on and on. How did it all happen? Where do I go from here?

But it was 3:13 in the morning and he had to find a way to get some sleep!

Today was the "Bible Boys," as his wife would call them. He had to force himself to show up, though most of the time, he couldn't believe how he acted in public: so unsure of himself, so tentative when he spoke, and sometimes, his skin seemed to tingle and his left arm felt numb. But he was going to be there in three hours, whether he slept or not!

the Pastor

Two and half-hours later, the 44 year old Pastor of Community Church was getting up also. Exhausted, he continued to think and re-think the Elders meeting the night before. It went on until 11:45 p.m.! *"How can I be so exhausted, and not be able to sleep?"* he thought. It was like so many of the other Elders meetings: contentious, suspicious, and with unspoken personal agendas which colored the tone of every glance, every expression, and every report.

This congregation really had two factions, two separate families trying to live in the same house. One family had built the house, and things were *"just fine."* The other family was trying to build a new life there, and thought things were *"not fine the way they were."*

The "older congregation" were the men and women who had literally raised the money and "built the church." These men and women had joined the church when the United States was the unparalleled manufacturer of world-class cars, stereos, TVs and steel. There was employment, stability, coherent families, and each man wore a tie on Sunday. Patterns and habits were clearer then.

The "younger congregation" was comprised of the men and women who grew up in the post WWII world of the sixties, seventies, eighties, and nineties. They were the "Baby Boomers" and the "Yuppies" who were raising kids in the "Generation X." They wanted to change some of the music, again, and they also wanted to modify the sanctuary to let in more light. And more radical yet, they wanted to start a "Christian day care"; even though the church budget was already in the red. Were these "new people" dreamers, scoundrels, or fools? Or were they the lifeblood and future of this small, now struggling, church?

So, the "contention du jour" was this once and future Christian Children's Day Care Center. For almost 20 years, as a way to pay the mortgage, the church had contracted with private groups to use the church's vacant buildings during the week for a commercial, for-profit day care center. The Community Church had received substantial rent, which amounted to one-third of the church's income. The Pastor and the "new people" felt that the Community Church needed to fill the buildings with Christian ministries, including a Christian day care center.

"If you don't have the money, you can't do it!" was the chant of the older congregation.

The Pastor had just turned 44 and had been fighting for his

"dream" for so long that he had thought it was simply that…a "dream." He wanted one thing…to lead people to Christ. But in those "old days" of criticism, he was fortunate to survive and remain "un-angry." His reaction to the criticism was to become very depressed. He sought counseling, attended support groups, and suffered through dark nights of the soul. As he tried to get out of bed that morning, he thought how he didn't like himself in those days, and said a short prayer that the "old days" would never come back.

In those days, he couldn't sleep either. In those days, he cried out to God to show him a way out of the quagmire known as the Community Church. He was in counseling trying to keep from falling into complete "stop" mode. He was battered by the criticisms of the very people that were supposed to follow him. He was supposed to be the beloved leader of his church, active and well known in the local community and among his pastoral colleagues. He was supposed to be held in a place of esteem. These people were supposed to be his flock. He was supposed to be their shepherd. He was supposed to be happy.

That morning was not as bad as it was in the "old days." Nothing could have been what it was like "before." He forced himself to recall the feelings of only 18 months ago. Nothing could be as bad as it was then. He couldn't beat his depression. He couldn't handle the infighting:

He was tired of the gossip and criticism:

> of him, his sermons, and his wife,
> of his clothes, his shoes, his cologne,
> of his office, his desk, his jokes,
> of being told that he was "too loving" and not "stern" enough,
> yet, being told by others, that he was too much in control and not "sensitive" enough,

of depending on the same old people, yet, not listening to them enough,

of not being in his office enough,

of not being out caring for the congregation enough,

of calling too many meetings, yet, making decisions without consulting enough with the "right people,"

of allowing people to talk too much, while still not allowing other people to talk enough,

of not taking charge and leading enough, yet, being "too bossy."

That particular morning, all the Pastor prayed for, was what he had prayed for during the "old days"… *"Oh Jesus, give me patience today, let your Spirit take away my anxieties,* and he added *"thank you Lord that the 'old days' of criticism are gone at least for the now."*

the Electronics Guy

He looked like his name sounded. Deeply proud of his Sicilian heritage, he was typically seen just about every place and every day of the week in a "tank top." The Electronics Guy was 39, but guessing his age was next to impossible. He sported a ponytail, which was about a foot long and "a little round belly that shook when he laughed like a bowl full of jelly." When it came to being on time, he was in a class by himself. Arriving on time was not part of his style. He had a life story that just about everyone had heard. Briefly, he was raised in a rather affluent town and was introduced to drugs at a very young age. Right after high school, the Navy provided a fertile field to start "dealing." Even though he had two small daughters, he was out in the "Twilight Zone" most nights and mornings for most of his naval career. Reducing, but not abandoning the habit well into his mid-thirties; he had been "clean" for about a year now.

It was easy to look at him and instantly write him off. The pony tail for starters. He would also talk at length and then some more, and then some more, about his life, or his three jobs, his Christian faith, his family and particularly his new granddaughter. But there was a side to him, which you couldn't help but love. He had stopped the drug habit, became committed to his family, Christ, his church, the Community Church, the music, ministry and, yes, a new multilevel marketing opportunity "the business." Well, the Electronics Guy was also getting up that morning, late as usual.

the International Banker

The next of the "Boys" waking up that morning was the International Banker, financier, and young 37 year old father. For anyone who knew the outside of the International Banker, one would think he had it "made." Living in a beautiful home, and dealing in international currency, he had a beautiful wife, two beautiful children, and presented a gentle spirit to the outside world. He was heard to be constantly traveling to some exotic international venues and trading several million dollars at a turn. He was particularly respected because he had available cash, which he offered to his church, the Community Church, but in a way that was not in the least way self-serving or braggadocios.

The International Banker's private side though, was quite different. His eldest son, a 7 year old had a bleeding retina. This was caused by the boy's body apparently rejecting it's own retina, causing his eye to bleed. The uncertainty of it all, the pain for his son, the possible blindness, the never-ending doctor's visits for his wife and son, all took their toll. In his private moments, the International Banker prayed that he would be given his son's pain and his son's blindness, rather than have his innocent boy and wife suffer more. He and his wife had decided to become "prayer warriors," so God would hear their prayers and let this pain and illness go away.

The International Banker left in plenty of time for the "Boys." As usual, he was to be one of the first to arrive, where it all began.

the Retired Salesman

The Retired Salesman was 78 years young and was also in route to the "Bible Boys." He had cared for his wife of 50 years, during an almost 10 year campaign against Alzheimer's disease. But he had lost her. He had almost died in the process. Now it was years later, and he had recently married his joyous and hard loving wife. He was exuberant in his love of Christ, his new church, and being able for the first time, in so very, very long, to have the companionship and love of a Christian woman. Rather than try to continue in either of their previous churches, they decided to launch into a new church, and recently joined the Community Church.

But all was not that great with the Retired Salesman either. He had an unknown ailment that caused irregular heartbeats. But what had become particularly painful lately, was a damaged disc in his spine. It caused shooting pain throughout his body, especially in his jaw. With the combination of a fragile heart and lightning bolts of pain shooting through his body, the 78 year old was running on the edge of life. Yet, not only did he not show it, he was exuberant about life and his many loves.

Study Guide –
Introduction to the Process of Self-Examination

This Small Group Study Guide is not like the usual "workbook," where the author provides lengthy and erudite biblical references that seem to provide answers. The goal of this Study Guide is to offer short open-ended questions which hopefully will stimulate discussion, debate, and candid sharing of feelings and thoughts wherein true self-reflection, self-education, and self-growth in understanding the Holy Spirit can take place.

Participants of Small Groups are encouraged, much like the six men in the story, to:

- be unrestrained about exploring the questions / challenges they may have,
- be bold in putting forth their understandings and opinions,
- not defer to those who seem to be the "biblical experts" in the room,
- make sense of things by listening to their own internal voice.

Typically, each chapter's study session will be at least an hour. Chapter Six is an exception as the number of, and depth of, questions clearly cannot be explored in one session. Let the needs of your members guide you in determining how many sessions to devote to Chapter Six.

Although each age has claimed it, these contemporary times are indeed unique, challenging, and that "ole time religion" doesn't seem to be working as well as it once did. Using self-reflection and group exploration through frank discussion, the provided Study Guide questions are designed to expand and challenge your thinking.

Study Guide – Chapter 1:
Starting Point – an introduction to the six men

Individual Reflection:

Take 15 minutes to quietly reflect and jot down your thoughts on the following:

1. Can you relate to the extreme difficulties experienced by any of the characters? If yes, briefly describe one such experience.
2. What were your thoughts/feelings, if any, about God the Father during this time of extreme difficulty?
3. What were your thoughts/feelings, if any, about Jesus Christ during this time of extreme difficulty?
4. What were your thoughts/feelings, if any, about the Holy Spirit during this time of extreme difficulty?
5. Has your connection/understanding/relationship to the three persons of the Trinity changed over the different stages/phases of your life? If yes, in what way?

Group Discussion/Share:

Address the above questions one at a time and, for those who wish to share, discuss your answers/insights.

CHAPTER 2

HOLY SPIRIT

Most of these "Bible Boys" sessions began with lots of jokes and laughs all around. Usually, there was a great deal of kidding, as the men got to pretend that they were younger, more virile, and more masculine than they could get away with in front of their wives. It got the brain moving in the morning trying to remember a punch line from some off-color joke or what was said in some Star Trek episode. Eventually, the late comers would trudge in, and the group tried to settle down and focus on what they were there for.

The Pastor would take the lead, *"O.K. where were we…could someone lead us in prayer."*

The High School Counselor obliged, *"Lord God, thank you for allowing us to meet together to try to learn more about your word. Be with us this morning as we try to live in a pleasing way before your power and majesty."*

The Pastor continued, *"O.K. thanks, now where did we leave off last week. Someone read John 16:7."*

The Electronics Guy read, *"But I tell you the truth, it is to your advantage that I go away; for if I do not go away, the helper shall not come to you; but if I go, I will send Him to you."*

The Pastor asked, *"O.K. What does that mean? Anybody?"*

After a rather lengthy silence, the Lawyer spoke up, *"Well it means that Christ's mission on earth had been completed and that He was returning to the Father in heaven."* He couldn't get over that no one else had spoken up, since he was almost parroting what he had learned in all his years of Catholic upbringing.

The Pastor asked, *"What does all this mean?"*

You really couldn't tell if the Pastor knew the answer by the way that he was asking the questions. But the Pastor was a gentle man. He had a soft way of talking about Christ. He was quite the intellectual, yet everything about him projected an attitude of don't look at me for answers. Let's find the answers together because if I tell you an answer it may not be of value to you, but if we can find the answer together, then we can share the truth and grow in our understanding.

The Retired Salesman, the senior of the group, and the International Banker remained in pensive moods. The Electronics Guy started to use the cross-reference in his Bible to come up with what he thought was the "best answer."

"What is it to indwell?" the Lawyer asked. *"Why don't you guys define your terms so we know what we are talking about?"*

So the Electronics Guy added-in, *James says, 'God has sent the Spirit of His Son into our hearts' in Galatians 4:6 and in 1 Corinthians 3:16-17."*[1]

"Is that why our bodies are to be considered the temple of the Holy Spirit?" asked the Pastor *"Is it because the Holy Spirit actually resides in our bodies?"*

Instantaneously, the Lawyer and the International Banker came to a frank and immediate realization…although they had both gone

---

[1] (Stanley, p.31, para. 2)

References to the Bible are from Charles Stanley's book, The Wonderful Spirit Filled Life, Thomas Nelson Publishers, Nashville. These biblical are inserted in the text here as an aid to the reader.

through Catholic grammar school and high school, and attended college, they had no clear idea what these guys were talking about.

They wondered, *"Who was the Holy Spirit anyway?"* Their minds ached for understanding.

The International Banker's heart ached for other reasons also. His "faith" would swing in somewhat extreme degrees. Sometimes it was clear that there was a kind and generous God, and he believed that God's promises were going to come true. But then there was this thing with his son's eye. How could a gentle and fair God allow an innocent child to suffer so? Now these guys were talking about a God within me. *"Come on guys – slow down."* he thought.

The Electronics Guy moved right through this discussion quite easily because he was like his Sicilian father who firmly believed that if God said it, it is true. So don't even question it. Period. He was anxious to demonstrate his new Bible. He had the "fully annotated" version and could find a biblical passage in record time. He loved to find the correct passage before the others, and by referring to the footnotes, could opine about various points from their analysis.

The Retired Salesman, quietly smiled to himself and thought that these youngsters were starting to stumble into one of the great mysteries of faith. But he knew also, that they had to make the journey by themselves. So he remained quiet, but couldn't help but smile.

The Retired Salesman's life was at a low point during his late wife's last few years of health. It was then that he couldn't cope. His wife was slipping into death. His own heart was failing from the stress and anxiety. He couldn't go forward or backward. So he turned to prayer. He believed that prayer was the answer, and he had confidence that whatever the outcome of his heart problem or his painful damaged disc, it would be the will of God. So why worry?

The Pastor instantaneously reflected back to his truth, back to the "old days." When he actually believed he faced the prospects of losing his church. But this morning, he was convinced that the "troops" were marching in the right direction, so he just let them march on.

The Lawyer was lost in thought: with the problems of his practice, and his ice cold feet all the time, he was actually enjoying the mental gymnastics of the discussion. He loved the challenge of all these "biblical scholars," and wanted to probe deeper into what they were talking about. Could these experts explain it all, even to themselves?

He asked, *"So what is the Holy Spirit supposed to be doing, guys?"*

Some instantly visualized the dove sitting on top of the apostle's heads.

But that couldn't be it?

Could it?

The High School Counselor was much more at ease than the rest. He thought back as to how he discussed the subject of the Holy Spirit with his junior high school students, and said

"Guys, the Holy Spirit is one of the Trinity, who is just as powerful, resourceful, and awesome as God the Father and Jesus Christ. He is actually alive inside each one of us, if we let him. If we don't, then, forget it. So there's definitely a choice here. It is a recognition, a releasing, a letting go, of what it is that makes each one of you, you. And it is a giving up of control over your own life."

The men experienced various thoughts.

"Oh that's just great, just peachy! Here we are, trying to make decisions, decisions about our families, about our careers, our children, our marriages, to do what Jesus taught us to do, and this young High School Counselor tells us that we have to give up control!"

"What if we give up control? Doesn't it necessarily follow that we may, or may not, make the decisions that God would want us to make?"

"This is not logical. You've got to give up control to get control over your life?"

"Easy to say. You deal with young kids all the time, but the rest of us have to live in the cold hard world and if you don't take control over your life, you might as well forget it. You'll get eaten up!"

Study Guide – Chapter 2:
Holy Spirit

Individual Reflection:

Take 15 minutes to quietly reflect and jot down your thoughts on the following:

1. What is your current understanding of the Holy Spirit?
2. What questions do you have about the Holy Spirit?

Group Discussion/Share:

Address the above questions one at a time and, for those who wish to share, discuss your answers/insights.

CHAPTER 3

DOUBTS, GUILT, ANGER

The Pastor popped in, *"And it's all set forth in the Bible. Here's the big picture; Jesus came into our world and died for us and in that process he paid for our sins. He allowed us to step out of our in-born sinfulness. He also taught us how to live. He demonstrated how He wants us to live: both in our actions and in our thoughts."*

"*Has anyone noticed, that the standard Jesus established for us is a little bit difficult to live up to"* the Pastor asked?

The Lawyer's mind flashed to the first time that he heard that phrase about turning the "other cheek." He remembered thinking, *"What are you crazy! It'd never work! You'd get massacred in this world!"*

The International Banker thought about his least favorite Bible story; the one about giving everything you own away and come follow me. *"How can that possibly work?"* he thought.

The Retired Salesman quickly thought back to his inability to accept the death of his first wife. He was supposed to deal with it with "a kind and Christian heart," but he knew in the quiet recesses of his heart that he was still angry at God for allowing his wife to suffer. Ten years is a long time to suffer the small debilitating erosion of everything that makes a person a person. Having a spouse, a loved and loving friend, a life's partner, eaten away a snip at a time is the cruelest form of punishment. It is not only a frustration and embarrassment to the afflicted one; it is a chipping away of the caregiver, piece by piece, day after day, year after year. As we know, Alzheimer's is the disease that not only kills the patient; it kills the caregiver as well. *"Christ told us to forgive and move on with life,"* he thought, *"but how can God be forgiven for doing that? How can I bring myself to accept her experiencing such a terrible, terrible death? I know that I "should" but sometimes I just can't."* He suddenly turned sad and introspective. He was looking at himself square in the face, and not liking what he saw.

The Electronics Guy still felt burdened and guilty about all the years he wasted on drugs, and could not forgive himself; even though he knew that Jesus said *"forgive others, forgive yourself."* He was just plain angry when he looked at himself sometimes. He still became critical of his wife in public and angry with his friends if things did not go his way. Even though he had been "clean" for a couple of years, the anger came back all too often. He knew it, but it flashed up so quickly sometimes, without warning, that he just did not know what to do with it or about it. He had tried counseling and thought it worked for a time. But the anger would rage back again like a wild fire, without warning. At that moment, he also felt the weight of failure. Failure because he knew that he had failed to live up to the standard of Jesus. He felt spent, weakened, and he became unusually quiet.

The International Banker was feeling overwhelmed by the thought of his son's illness and suffering. Right then, he was feeling particularly depressed, spread in a thousand directions. He felt just plain down on himself. Things were not going along with his prayer wishes. He and his wife had become "prayer warriors" for his son's eye treatments, but things were simply not happening the way they were supposed to. The boy's body was continuing to reject his retina.

A trip was being arranged to take the seven year old to the

National Eye Institute in Bethesda Maryland. There were specialists there for this particular eye condition. The local Children's Hospital, the University Medical Center all could do nothing. As the number of experts who had looked at the case went up and up, the number of options went down and down. The trip to Bethesda could be the one last hope for any kind of normal life for his son. The trip would require his wife to stay there with the boy, by herself, for several weeks after the operation. Soon after the procedure, he had to be in South America on business.

He had so many questions.

- *"How could God do this to my family?"*
- *"How is my wife going to be able to hold up, alone 3,000 miles from family and friends?"*
- *"How could God let this happen after all those prayers?"*

The entire Community Church would pray regularly for his son's eye. He was sick at heart because nothing was working.

Then there was the Lawyer. Exhausted physically, emotionally, and spiritually, he was hanging on to the conversation, as he was hanging on to his life, at a moment by moment pace.

His sense of concentration had slipped. He found himself repeating the same conversation with himself, the same one that he had at 3:13 a.m. (over four hours earlier). His memory was slipping, telephone numbers went blank in his mind, and his job search had turned into one of great fear and disappointment. He and his wife were constantly considering pulling up stakes and returning to the family homestead back East. He did not know if he was "coming or going." He felt like he was floating, tired, and depressed.

The Pastor quietly thought of his continuing struggle to resist blasting away at the "establishment" in the congregation. He knew that he had to fight with his natural tendency to resent the ringleaders of the "establishment." They were in perceived positions of "power" and "prestige," and they simply did not want to give up that perceived standing and control. But he knew also that this was not what Jesus wanted him to do with his life.

He wondered why he could not get control over his life. It all raced through his mind again:

"The day care should be a disciple-maker, not a money maker!" they'd challenge.

Some of the "older congregation" felt the Pastor was being irresponsible with the church's financial future, and would challenge him on his lack of business savvy.

"How many successful businesses have you operated?" they'd ask.

He'd shoot back, *"About as many successful churches as you've pastored!"* all the while, not pleased with the taste of his verbal vengeance.

He and the "younger congregation" felt the church must put into practice the "Great Commission" (go and make disciples) as the first priority, and trust God to provide the financial and other resources.

"Faith first, then money! Money follows faithfulness, not the other way around." he would plead.

"We're not arguing against faith. We're arguing against foolishness!" would be the retort.

"We cannot afford not to do it!" he would argue. And on and on it would go, ad-nauseum.

The High School Counselor still harbored a deep resentment toward the Principal, a loathing of the man, which did not seem to subside, no matter how hard he prayed and tried to forgive.

He flashed back to when he and the other employees took their claims to the high school's Board of Directors, and then to the Regional Council. The employees, nine out of ten, signed written statements about the emotional illness of the Principal. To each employee's credit, they wanted to get professional treatment for the Principal and not to have him removed from his job.

The High School Counselor, along with the other eight staff members, had prepared written statements of their observations of the Principal during the preceding 12 months. The time came when he, just like the other staff members, was "on the outs' with the Principal. These were "the dead days of the soul" for this young counselor. Often the Principal spoke to him about the need for him to use his gifts in ways other than working with young people. He started to slide further into a loss of self-confidence, anxiety, and over time, weight loss and depression. There was a feeling of being hopelessly lost somewhere in his life.

Ultimately, after almost a year, the feelings of confusion and depression turned into white-hot feelings of resentment and anger. He became determined, along with the other eight staff of the school, to open the veil of illness and deception being practiced so methodically by the Principal. The pattern of the Principal's illness became clearer than ever.

The High School Counselor flashed back to three occasions when he confronted the Principal about spreading false accusations to the School Board members. On two of them, some of the people to whom the Principal had made these false statements were actually present when the Principal flatly denied having ever said them. The Counselor understood that the Principal was not out-and-out lying, but rather was having difficulty recalling and processing reality.

But the High School Counselor also flashed back to the feelings of abandonment and helplessness he felt along with the other eight employees in seeking the intervention of the Regional Council. He knew he harbored deep, deep wounds that he had not recovered from. How could he? The feelings were larger than he could handle.

At that moment, the truth of the "Bible Boys" was self-evident:

failure, disorientation, and shame. Each man, in his own private way, was not living up to what Jesus wanted.

There was a very long pause. Everyone seemed lost in thought.

Eventually, the Lawyer said, *"Guys, does anyone have a clue as to what the Holy Spirit is supposed to be doing in this mess?"*

Study Guide – Chapter 3:
Doubts, Guilt, Anger

Individual Reflection:

Take 15 minutes to quietly reflect and jot down your thoughts on the following:
Reflecting on a time of doubt, guilt, and/or anger in your life:

1. What were your thoughts/feelings about God the Father, if any, during this time of doubt, guilt, and/or anger?
2. What were your thoughts/feelings about Jesus Christ, if any, during this time of doubt, guilt, and/or anger?
3. What were your thoughts/feelings about the Holy Spirit, if any, during this time of doubt, guilt, and/or anger?

Group Discussion/Share:

Address the above questions one at a time and, for those who wish to share, discuss your answers/insights.

CHAPTER 4

RELATIONSHIPS

The High School Counselor's mind flashed back to what had transpired. His thoughts invoked such intense feelings of a whole range of emotions and experiences: abuse of theology, manipulation of power, "blindness" of the board members, and the almost powerless influence of the Regional Council in charge of oversight. He came to learn that when an appointed leader has a serious emotional illness, there is little help to be had from the "respected and responsible authorities."

He learned deep inside his heart that those who are supposed to be watching and making sure that everything comes out right in the end…aren't!

His personal crisis started in such a strange way. Kate, his friend and director of the High School Center, called him about the newly arrived Principal who changed the locks inside the Center five times during his first week on the job! What could be so important about the locks?

Next, there was that strange trip to the Principal's former home several hours drive away. The Principal asked the High School Counselor to cut his lawn. He did it, but it sure was strange to drive several hours away to cut a lawn. It was then that their first "private conversation" took place.

The Principal confided, *"Don't you see that there are a few members of staff, like Kate, that are not cut out to be in their jobs? You see I am looking for people who want to be on my team. People who will trust me and let me get to know them, their hopes and dreams, what they and their families want, and what I can give them. But you must trust me and keep this conversation confidential."*

The High School Counselor later found out that in addition to Kate, the new Principal also told the Music Director, the Associate Principal, and the Administrative Secretary that they were all *"not cut out for their jobs."*

Then the Principal's memos started:

- *"To share about your life and help me to get to know you..."*
- *"What do you find rewarding, and what really excites you?"*
- *"What gives you joy in your work?"*

Then the "strange" memos began:

- *"Under no circumstances do I want to be discussed with another school board or staff member."*
- *"Under no circumstances are you to politic Board Members or other individuals for your benefit."*
- *"Let's work hard according to the gifts God has given us, let's try hard to be open with each other, and trust God to lead us according to His good plan."*

Initially, the High School Counselor was apparently "on the inside" with the Principal. All he could do was watch as his friends and peers withstood the wrath and penalties of being "on the outs" with the Principal. Watching it unfold, the High School Counselor couldn't help but slide into doubt, confusion and an inability to believe what he was seeing before his very own eyes.

Kate was the first target.

In response to the memo asking her to share about her life, Kate provided seven pages of open, and somewhat intimate, responses about her life, hopes, and goals. The Principal did not provide her any comment or reaction whatsoever. Kate felt invaded. Her most private inner thoughts were shared with her spiritual leader. He now knew something about her that few others did, yet...he provided no reaction, offered no help. It felt bad.

Then he denied her request to attend an annual teacher's conference, suggesting that she may not be doing that type of work anymore. He made a subtle reference that it may be "necessary" for her to be covered by her husband's insurance. *"What if there was a sudden drop in her income?"* he asked. The Principal summarily ignored her many memos about her projects, even those that had to do with the Christian education of the Center's youngsters. The Principal explained, *"The Board of Directors will give me a certain amount of money for staff, and I will create job descriptions and dollar values for each job."*

He asked her not to tell her husband of their conversations and to *"trust him"* alone to work it out. He said, *"You should not be scared, I will take care of you."* As each day passed, she felt more manipulated.

The office's secretary was next.

The Administrative Secretary had worked at the school for only about three weeks. Her experience was similar to that of Kate's.

The Administrative Secretary felt that the Principal's behavior seemed irrational because there was no reason given for the constant changes. The Principal would change routines, deadlines, workload, and assignments in reference to the other staff members, on a daily basis, sometimes hourly. Her own job description seemed to change from day to day.

The Principal called the Administrative Secretary into his office, closed the door, and told her that Kate was *"pathologically disturbed,"* and that Kate would not be remaining in her position. There was no reason to share this information with the Administrative Secretary. The Principal's erratic behavior was becoming more irrational. Before long, the Administrative Secretary started to doubt herself.

The Principal told her a story about a previous secretary who was incompetent. Then he would call the Administrative Secretary by the previous secretary's name. He would regularly tell her that her skills weren't up to par, but that he would train her. Next he would send her a formal letter or quick note praising her skills and demeanor. She never really knew how he actually felt about her job performance or her as an individual.

The High School Counselor was aware of all this and these events raced through his mind. He thought about what the Principal had done to him, but then he quickly caught himself and returned to the conversation with the "Bible Boys."

Study Guide – Chapter 4:
Relationships

Individual Reflection:

Take 15 minutes to quietly reflect and jot down your thoughts on the following:

1. Have you ever had a boss or been in a relationship with someone who was dysfunctional? If yes, briefly describe the experience.
2. What were your thoughts/feelings about God the Father, if any, during the time in this relationship?
3. What were your thoughts/feelings about Jesus Christ, if any, during the time in this relationship?
4. What were your thoughts/feelings about the Holy Spirit, if any, during the time in this relationship?

Group Discussion/Share:

Address the above questions one at a time and, for those who wish to share, discuss your answers/insights.

CHAPTER 5

CONTROL

The Lawyer continued, *"How many of you guys think you can pull off what Jesus asked by yourselves?"*

Everyone answered in his own mind that he couldn't, and it wasn't even close.

The Pastor flashed back to his moment of truth and what it meant to him.

Back in the old days, he was getting a divorce, half the church members were quitting on that count alone, and the other half were unhappy with his sermons and just about everything else they could think of. Church membership was dropping and the cash coffers were never so low.

He wasn't happy with the sermons either. He found myself, without even realizing it, giving his sermons to try to keep the minority happy. He would make copious notes of what he was supposed to say for fear of offending someone. He was afraid all the time. Afraid of the "establishment," afraid of what his divorce would do to his career, afraid that he was losing everything, afraid that he would end up as an unemployed minister at the age of 42.

The Pastor was a broken man then: experiencing a divorce he

didn't want, a depression he couldn't accept, and dysfunction he couldn't change. All this had undone him.

One afternoon, he went into the sanctuary to "work out some things" with God. Like a hundred times before, he pleaded for a spiritual revival to come upon his church. He was angry with God for not doing what he wanted God to do. He was angry at the church for not doing what God wanted to do. He was angry with himself because it must all be his fault.

But, he had also heard *"let go, and let God."* So he offered his dreams and hopes and desires for this church to God. He started to cry. All he could do was mouth the words without a sound.

> *"Jesus, I quit, I am no longer the pastor here. All my work and prayers and words I offer on this altar to you. I cannot make the people trust in you. I cannot make them desire your Word. I cannot make them want to enjoy you in prayer. I cannot make them want to come to worship you. I have tried, and I cannot grow this church. I have tried, and this congregation is no different than when I came here. I know Moses didn't quit when his people fought him, but I can't go on. You've got to forgive me if this is a sin, but I can't go on.*
>
> *I had such dreams for this church, but they refused to see. So I guess they were just my dreams and not yours. I've tried, but I cannot do this, so I quit. You be the pastor, and you take care of them. Into your hands I commend this church."*

In the months that followed, the church did shake. Esteemed "pillars" of the church left in heated disgust, but instead of the church collapsing, it prospered. He preached like never before, with a new assurance and boldness. Longtime "pew potatoes" started having conversations right there in worship! Men began going to men's conferences and came back almost unrecognizable to their wives, *"What happened to him? He wants to pray with me, go to church with me, he helps with the dishes…he even wants to talk to me! What did you do to him?"*

Women went to women's conferences and for the first time heard womanhood defined in Biblical terms of wholesomeness, health, and strength. Early morning Bible studies, intercession ministries, midweek evening Bible studies, and healing dreams and visions broke loose throughout the entire congregation. Many members even began to tithe. *"The last part of a man's anatomy to be converted is his wallet!"* he preached.

Left and right, young and old, black and white, newcomer and old, all were awakened by this wave of the Spirit shaking the church; however, those not caught up in the Spirit had a different perspective:

- *"In my 37 years as a faithful member of this church, I have never seen a pastor create such crisis, controversy and division as he does!"*
- *"Our traditional service is dying, and that praise service with all that loud music and those people are taking over."*
- *"The pastor is becoming an extremist, preaches for 30 or 40 minutes, and always about Jesus and the Bible."*
- *"We must talk to his denominational superiors about him."*
- *"All the committee meetings have got to be on the same night of the month, just so they could have their prayer meetings. This means I can only be on only one committee."*
- *"He is out teaching Bible studies and anointing babies when he should be visiting the shut-ins and attending committees, doing the work of the church."*
- *"I have to make an appointment just to talk with him!"*
- *"He is ignoring the very wishes of the people who hired him!"*
- *"And these new people, I don't think they should have as much say in the church as the rest of us."*

- "Half of the people who built this church are leaving, and what are the elders doing about it."
- "Who is going to pay the bills? When the pastor doesn't get a raise at the New Year, he'll see."
- "And what does he mean by a "Christian" day care, anyway?"
- "Let's circulate a petition to get rid of him."
- "This is the worst crisis we've ever had, and the pastor is a fool for creating such turmoil in his own church!"
- "The direction the pastor is taking is out of touch with what we want. It's obvious he is either unable or unwilling to listen to us, so we need to replace him."

He came out of these thoughts and finally spoke to the "Bible Boys."

"I remember sitting alone in the chapel for hours at a stretch, and then one time I finally had reached the end of my rope and said to God: This is it, I can't do it, I do not have the skill, power, intelligence or whatever it takes to pull this thing off, so you can have this church and everything that's in it. I give up!"

"So what happened?" one of the boys asked.

The Pastor continued, "Well, I believe in the deep recesses of my heart, God spoke to me and led me to His Spirit. I realized what I had been overlooking. I was outright forgetting about the Holy Spirit.

I remembered that simple passage from the Bible where Jesus said that He was going to the Father, and to not be afraid because the Holy Spirit would come to those who ask and to those who want and need help. You don't need to be in control, but rather to give up control to God. The Holy Spirit is within us. And if we give up that control, we can get the help we need to live the life that Jesus asks of us.

Basically guys, if you try to pull this off by yourself, you might as well forget it, but with the help of the Holy Spirit, we have a fighting chance."

Study Guide – Chapter 5:
Control

Individual Reflection:

Take 15 minutes to quietly reflect and jot down your thoughts on the following:

1. What are your thoughts/feelings about "control" in your life?
2. Remembering a time of extreme difficulty in your life, what did you think/feel then about controlling the situation?
3. What were your thoughts/feelings, if any, about how God the Father worked with you to control the situation, if at all?
4. What were your thoughts/feelings, if any, about how Jesus Christ worked with you to control the situation, if at all?
5. What were your thoughts/feelings, if any, about how the Holy Spirit worked with you to control the situation, if at all?

Group Discussion/Share:

Address the above questions one at a time and, for those who wish to share, discuss your answers/insights.

.

CHAPTER 6

DWJWD!

The Pastor continued, *"We want to be in control, that's our nature, but none of us has what it takes. We aren't built that way. We are a mishmosh of strange stuff, and it is only when we realize it, accept it and deeply, deeply accept our lack of control, and acknowledge that without the Holy Spirit, we can do nothing. That's right - absolutely nothing! The Holy Spirit is not some pigeon flying around out there. He is as equally powerful as God the Father and Jesus Christ, and He is within each one of us now, and without the Holy Spirit, we cannot even hope to do what Jesus has asked us to do. Think about that!"*

The Retired Salesman added, *"You have to find a way to quiet your mind boys. Everybody has to find their own way – but if you do not quiet your mind, you can't possibly listen. It always hits me that so many people say things like: 'Let's pray that the Spirit will be with us here today.' Gentleman, I believe that the Holy Spirit is with each of us 24/7, but it is us who do not quiet our minds and listen. It is us who don't 'let the Spirt be with us' not the other way around. It's like —the Holy Spirit came down—and never left! If you believe the Bible and in Jesus, then you have to believe that the Holy Spirit is with us and in us."*

The High School Counselor offered, *"You know I get up every morning and I read two passages in the Bible, and I sorta make a plan to do something that day with what I read. It's like, it's not just about my do-to-list but about what am I supposed to be doing based on what I read. Then I say — thank you God for being in my back pocket for this day."*

The Electronics Guy, *"Man I would look at myself at the end of the day and say "Man I did nothing for God today." Then I realized that this was just plain stupid, so I started to think of all the little things I did throughout the day and then asked myself …. 'Did I honor God today?', and you know what? …I did!"*

Then the Lawyer, *"Ok let's say that's true, what's the Holy Spirit telling us anyway?"*

The Pastor, *"Well, we all know: WWJD? What Would Jesus Do? What a wonderful simple, even elegant way to remember the question to ask ourselves."*

The Lawyer, *"I sure don't want to be contrary, but wait a minute, you could ask yourself that question over and over all day long and it would not lead to actually doing anything. What's the point if you don't actually do anything about it? Anyone can know what to do, but never do anything about it."*

The International Banker: *"You know I was raised by a Cherokee mom and she was never so much into me 'being saved' as she was into 'how much work was I doing for others'"*

The Electronics Guy, *"I prefer: WDJD. What Did Jesus Do? Clearly I need to learn what Jesus did. I believe that God wants us is to enter into a relationship with Christ and immerse ourselves in that relationship. To do that, I have to devote myself to the study of the Bible, so that's what I'm doing. I'm an engineer, so I want to know how God works and reading the Word helps me understand, but this group is giving me a different perspective."*

The International Banker, *"What gets me is that I know people, and I'm sure you guys do too, that apparently have no relationship with God or Jesus, no connection to a church, but who are the most giving people I know. Yet I know people that go to church, but that's all they do."*

The Lawyer asks rhetorically, *"Am I always the one disagreeing?"* and continues, *"The way I see it, I can study and study and be in small groups and read and read, but all that does not lead me to actually doing anything. It's like we've heard the pastor say. 'The three persons of God are not the Father, Son and Holy Scriptures.' You know the difference between doing something and not doing something? Well...it's doing something."*

The International Banker, *"Ok. Ok. I got it: How about DWJD? – Do What Jesus Did! We are supposed to do what Jesus did, right? You know 'feed the hungry,' 'bring health to communities.' Isn't that what we're supposed to be doing?"*

The Electronics Guy, *"You've got to be kidding! Hey, I'm just a regular normal human here. Jesus was God, powerful, able to do miracles and all that. I can't do what Jesus did. No way, we're not even in the same league!"*

The Lawyer, *"I wonder if even the Apostles felt powerful enough to do what Jesus did."*

The International Banker, *"Actually, what gives me hope is that the Apostles were such losers! Think about it. If Christ turned His kingdom over to the likes of them, then there may be some hope for me. They managed to do His work after He left, so there's hope that I can too."*

The High School Counselor, *"I spend a lot of time with kids and, even at such a young age, they have a strong fear of failure. It paralyzes them. I tell them...the line between winning and losing, between success and failure is really a very thin line. If they just push through the fear, they can move forward."*

The Electronics Guy, *"It's sorta like faith."*

The Pastor, *"Yes! The line you cross for Jesus. It's not a big line! You just have to push through and take action.*

The Lawyer: *"Ok. OK. I've got it! How about DWJWD? Do What Jesus Would Do? That's a real call to action. It's simple, easy to understand, easy to remember, direct. Is it the message from the Holy Spirit? I think, yes it is! This is the Holy Spirt talking to me with an exclamation point! Telling me to keep Jesus in mind and then do something! Take action!*

It's not a question, like WWJD. What Would Jesus Do? It's not a statement, like WDJD. What Did Jesus Do; which sounds like a history class. It's an Exclamation Point! Do What Jesus Would Do! It's an expression of joy, of confidence, and it is a call to action."

The Electronics Guy. *"I like this! One question…do we DWJWD by chance or do we plan to DWJWD each day?"*

The Retired Salesman: *"I think we have to be intentional about it. Let me tell you a story about something that changed my perspective. My wife and I went on an overnight church retreat, and the one thing that sticks out in my mind from the experience is the image of a three legged stool that we talked about. The seat part is our faith, and the three legs are: Piety, Christian Study, and Christian Action. Sometimes in our lives the stool gets wobbly because we focus too much on one of the legs and not enough on the others. When this happens our faith gets off balance. Luckily the Holy Spirit is with us, nagging us to not forget about the other legs."*

The Pastor: *"The image that sticks with me is of a cross. The vertical axis is our relationship with God—— but the horizontal axis —that's about our relationships with other people – and you can't have that relationship with them unless you reach out –and actually do something with them or for them."*

The Retired Salesman: *"Boys, Christian life is like dancing. You know when you are dancing you sorta have to feel what your partner is doing, the slightest subtle move or pressure will guide you if you are open to it. I guess you can dance by the numbers and set steps and be mechanical about it, but the great dancers are those that flow with their partners to the music, being responsive, being open, being active, and physical about it; doing the do, having fun and happiness".*

The Electronics Guy: *"That's just terrific – I'm a crummy dancer!"*

The Retired Salesman: *"Wait a minute; wait a minute. I didn't say Christian life didn't take some effort and some thought and some practice. That's where prayer comes in. You know the great Coach Vince Lombardi of the Green Bay Packers? He said 'Practice doesn't make perfect. Perfect Practice makes perfect.' Prayer is like that. Like I said before, you have to quiet your mind, listen and feel, be open and practice on a daily basis. If you don't, then how can you hear the Holy Spirit or ever take action to Do What Jesus Would Do?"*

The Lawyer: *"I guess my version would be in legal terms. Get off your Ass–ets! You know what I mean? It's like in legal terms, am I sitting on my assets? I'm convinced in that old saying 'Evil can only succeed when men of good will do nothing.' Another way to think about it…evil can only succeed if men of good will take too long studying something and never get around to doing anything about it. I think the Holy Spirit is basically saying…Get off your Ass–ets!"*

The International Banker: *"You know, as a banker, I'm the guy who likes to play by the rules; but as I think about this DWJWD, the more convinced I am that I have been taking the easy way out. Sometimes following the rules is a lot like following the crowd, always fitting into the stereo types, showing up just like I'm supposed to show up, following everyone's expectations. But what the Holy Spirit is saying is that I am supposed to be busting out of the "normal," the "regular," and DWJWD!*

Looking at the Lawyer… *"You know, I think I'm going to get off my Ass–ets." and Do What Jesus Would Do, as of today!"*

The Retired Salesman: *"The thing that really bothers me about all this is that our culture these days seems to pit people against people. People augur into their own stupidity whether it's Republican versus Democrat, or black versus police, gun control versus 2nd amendment, hell, the list goes on and on because they are all so judgmental and sure of themselves. If we don't learn to listen to the other guy and try to understand where they are coming from then we will relegate our lives deeper and deeper into our own closed minded hole. Remember when Jesus came upon the harlot being stoned? What did he do? Was he closed minded? No! He listened! He listened to the people with the stones, and then he listened to the woman. Jesus talked to both sides. Gosh, I wish I were a better listener."*

The Electronics Guy: *"Do you guys think the Holy Spirit has a different message for each person? If it's true, it is probably why there is such hatred in the world and in our neighborhoods — everyone thinks that God has a unique, personal message or commandment that speaks just to them, and supports their world view. It's why terrorists blow up innocent people without the slightest remorse, and why we talk behind the pastor's back about what is best for our church. We are convinced that we have the one and only true message from God which makes us right and the other guy wrong. It can't be this way; can it? If it is, people will remain divided, us against them: Democrats versus Republicans, blacks versus whites, Catholics versus Jews versus Protestants versus Muslims. Yikes! This is so depressing."*

The Lawyer: *"Come on…who actually believes that God makes personalized, customized, totally unique messages for each one of us?"*

The High School Counselor: *"A lot of people think this, at least some of the time. How often do we make a decision based on some "sign" we receive and interpret as God's direction? A couple of years ago, when I had had it with the church, I walked away from it, but then I asked God… 'Okay, now what?' Around this time, an opportunity came up to become a High School Counselor, and I took it as a sign, and as you guys know, all these years later, that's what I do. I work with kids—and intend to do it for the rest of my life. Was becoming a High School Counselor a message from God? I don't know, but at the time it felt like one to me, and it led me down a path that improved my life."*

The Retired Salesmen: *"Rather than a direct messaging system, I see it more like a partnership boys. You know like in business. You have probably all been in partnerships. Hell, if you're married you are in a partnership for sure. What do partners do? They depend on each other. They cover for each other. They talk and share with each other. Hell, they love each other! That's what I think our relationship with the Holy Spirit is all about. It's a partnership, if you accept it."*

The Retired Salesman continuing: *"And like all relationships, it's a partnership you have to work at. You have to spend time listening and being open to the Holy Spirit to keep the relationship strong. You boys know that one about: 'Is your glass half-empty or half-full?' Well boys, when you are in partnership*

*with the Holy Spirit and DWJWD is central to your heart, then you are run-
ning at least 3/4 full. Life may not be easy, but you have hope. DWJWD is
your path, your guide, your light, and no matter what life throws at you you're
going to be able to handle it at least 3/4 full, and that's where you wanna be!"*

The High School Counselor: *"The question to ask ourselves is: What
are we doing to stay connected?"*

The Lawyer: *"I have this woman who cuts my hair and she always tells
me: 'If you were to die today, when you get up to the Pearly Gates someone is
going to ask you: What did you do with your life? Not…What did you learn?
Not…What did you think about? Not how smart were you on the bible, but
simply and directly…What did you actually do?!' You know that bit about 'to
those who have been given much, much will be asked?' Well boys, I sure as hell
hope I have a good answer to that question. She always says: 'You know, at that
moment, you'll be alone – the cavalry's not coming!'"*

Suddenly the Pastor, speaking with great force and seemingly
out of the blue: *"If the church "establishment" likes my action, great; if
they don't, they don't! The voice of the Holy Spirit is so clear and simple, if I
just remove all the stress, worry, clutter, and noise out of my head. This is what
I was missing! The Holy Spirit has been calling me this way all along; I just
needed to listen, but listening is the hard part. Guys, I wasn't listening, that's
why I have been lost."*

Everyone sat there for a moment, just quiet…a bit shocked.

The Lawyer, with a hearty slap on the Pastor's back, breaks the
silence: *"Now you've got it! The Holy Spirit been saying it all along…Do
What Jesus Would Do!"*

The Pastor, speaking with newly found clarity: *"It all makes sense
and I can show you guys where in the Bible this is all laid out. Turn to Acts
1:4-8."*

*"And gathering them together, He commanded them not to leave
Jerusalem, but to wait for what the Father has promised. For John*

baptized you with water, but you shall be baptized with the Holy Spirit not many days from now. You shall receive power when the Holy Spirit has come upon you; and you shall be my witnesses both in Jerusalem, and in all Judea and Samaria, and even to the remotest part of the earth.[2]

---

[2] (Stanley, p.9, para. 3)

References to the Bible are from Charles Stanley's book, The Wonderful Spirit Filled Life, Thomas Nelson Publishers, Nashville. These biblical are inserted in the text here as an aid to the reader.

Study Guide – Chapter 6:
DWJWD!

Individual Reflection:

Take 15 minutes (in each agreed upon session) to quietly reflect and jot down your thoughts on the assigned questions for that session's discussion.

1. What do you personally see as the difference between each of the below?

   - WWJD? *(What would Jesus do?)*
   - WDJD? *(What did Jesus do?)*
   - DWJWD? *(Do What Jesus Would Do!)*

2. Like the Retired Salesman, do you believe that *"You have to find a way to quiet your mind…if you do not quiet your mind, you can't possible listen."*? Do you quiet your mind before you pray? How?

3. Like the Retired Salesman, do you believe that the Holy Spirit is with *"each of us 24/7"*? Do you interact with the Holy Spirit throughout the day? How?

4. Like the High School Counselor, on the top of your to-do list, do you make a list of things each day to DWJWD? What have you done lately to DWJWD?

5. Like the Electronics Guy, do you evaluate your day as to how well you DWJWD? If you are off track, how do you course correct?

6. What do you think about the Lawyer's argument that the Holy Spirit is calling us to action? If you were to regard DWJWD as a personal command to you for action, how would that change what you do each day?

7. Do you think/feel that you need Biblical references for understanding DWJWD? What Bible verses can you point to that explain DWJWD?

8. As described by the Retired Salesman, what are the three legs of Faith?

9. As described by the Pastor, why is the cross a useful symbol of DWJWD?

10. How do you agree/disagree with the Lawyer regarding; *"Get off your ass—ets."*?

11. How do you agree/disagree with the International Banker about *"Busting out of the normal?"*

12. How do you agree/disagree with the Retired Salesman that *"when you are in partnership with the Holy Spirit and DWJWD is central to your heart, then you are running at least ¾ full."* What does running at least ¾ full look like for you?

13. How do you agree/disagree with the Electronics Guy that the Holy Spirit has a unique personalized message just for you?

14. How do you agree/disagree with the Retired Salesman's thinking – that our relationship with the Holy Spirit is a partnership, and like all relationships it's a partnership you have to work at. What will you do to strengthen your partnership with the Holy Spirit?

Group Discussion/Share:

Address the above questions one at a time and, for those who wish to share, discuss your answers/insights.

CHAPTER 7

EXPERIENCING THE HOLY SPIRIT

The Pastor asked, *"O.K. who doesn't get it?"*

"What you are saying is really reverse logic – you control your life only if you give up control of your life?" questioned the Lawyer.

Then the International Banker: *"O.K. we kind of know about the goodness of God the Father, we only have to look at the wonders of the world and of the life God has given us. Right? And we certainly know about Jesus, we have His life as a role model, we have the Bible as the written account of His life. Right? But what do we know about the Holy Spirit?*

The Pastor: *"Well guys I have a clever idea, why don't we look in the Bible and see for ourselves just what we do know about the Holy Spirit."*

The "boys" peruse their Bibles looking for relevant scripture. After a brief pause... *"O.K. what have you got?"*

"Well John 16:13 says; 'But when He, the Spirit of truth comes, He will guide you into all the truth.'"[3]

"1 Corinthians 2:11-12 also has something here: 'For who among men

---

[3] (Stanley, p.15, para. 2)

References to the Bible are from Charles Stanley's book, The Wonderful Spirit Filled Life, Thomas Nelson Publishers, Nashville. These biblical references are inserted in the text here as an aid to the reader.

knows the thoughts of a man except the spirit of the man, which is in him? Even so the thoughts of God no one knows except the Spirit of God. Now we have received, not the spirit of the world, but the Spirit who is from God, that we might know the things freely given to us by God."[4]

The Retired Salesman, sensing that the group wanted to hear from its senior member, *"Well it seems to me, that since the Holy Spirit is truly God then in some mysterious and magical way he is going to care for us and love us. We have to ask for his help just like we do of God the Father and Jesus Christ. It also seems to me that we have to be prepared to accept the pains of this life. We have to remember that just because we ask for something, it doesn't mean that we will get it!*

But here's a thought, how would you feel if you never got any respect or attention? If people forgot about you, didn't see you, recognize you, or ask for your help. If they don't give you the respect, love, and adoration that you deserve. That would feel pretty lousy if you ask me. You and I know we are supposed to pray to God the Father and to Jesus Christ. Don't you think the same applies to the Holy Spirit? The Spirit is telling us 24/7: DWJWD! Do What Jesus Would Do!"
Yes, I believe it, but we have to listen and we can't listen if we don't connect."

It was as if, all of a sudden, flash bulbs of recognition started popping all over the place. The Pastor settled back in his chair. There was a lot of head scratching and chin pulling as the Electronics Guy, the Lawyer, the International Banker, the Retired Salesman, the High School Counselor and even the Pastor clicked into "thought mode" in terms of each of their own stories.

Could the Electronics Guy ask the Holy Spirit to free him from his guilt about the drugs? And in that second, right there, right then, he saw a glimpse out of his guilt. It's O.K. that I can't do it myself.

---

[4] (Stanley, p.17, para. 7, p.18, para 6)
References to the Bible are from Charles Stanley's book, The Wonderful Spirit Filled Life, Thomas Nelson Publishers, Nashville. These biblical references are inserted in the text here as an aid to the reader.

I don't have to justify myself to my friends and peers, to my wife or my children. I can ask the Holy Spirit to release me from my guilt. I'll *Do What Jesus Would Do* today! I always thought that if I did things to make up for my past, then this feeling of guilt would go away. No, I don't have to do that anymore.

The International Banker flashed on how this all related to his son. Oh Holy Spirit, help me to accept my son's situation without losing my faith in you, turning to anger and resentment and being a disservice to you, my son, and my wife. Today, this minute, this hour, this day I'll *Do What Jesus Would Do!* Help me to release to you, to give up my false sense of being in control of my life and my son's life. Please show me how to comfort my wife and son in the uncertain days ahead of us. Bring me the peace that is yours through the example and teachings of Jesus. Yes! I can start right now, *Do What Jesus Would Do!* In that moment came a brief snapshot of a sense of peace he had not known before. Maybe being a "prayer warrior" was not the way.

The Lawyer was awed into silence. This was the most remarkable conversation that he had ever heard. Then he asked, *"Now let me get this straight guys, I give up control, so that I can give control of my life over to the Holy Spirit? I Do What Jesus Would Do in every situation possible, even the ugly ones, even with those crooked lawyers, and the broken system of the courts, and the result of all this is that I can find the peace that has eluded me for so long?"*

"What happens if it doesn't work?" he said to himself.

He thought for a moment and realized that he could not handle all this information at one time. He would talk it over with his wife. He didn't think it was beyond his comprehension, but he felt he needed to *"sleep on it,"* as his father would say. It was like his mind understood the concept, but without his heart fully and totally embracing the concept; it wouldn't stick. He wanted to make the leap into this world of giving up a sense of control over his life and *Do What Jesus*

Would Do. He thought that if he could talk it over with his wife, then it would become clearer to him, and in that clarity he could more fully and completely embrace the role of the Holy Spirit in his life.

The Pastor spoke next: *"Yeah, what is this new found relationship with the Holy Spirit like? Remember guys, it is not like you relate to the Holy Spirit like you relate to Jesus or God the Father. There are three distinct persons in one God, but each has separateness, a difference that you cannot forget. God the Father, the maker of the universe and of all that is good, is deserving of our adoration and worship with the majesty and honor that is only His. Jesus is our teacher, our role-model and our Savior. Without him, we would have never had our sins forgiven or known how to live in the first place. And now we have this new relationship with the Holy Spirit. What's it like?"*

Study Guide – Chapter 7:
Experiencing the Holy Spirit

<u>Individual Reflection:</u>
Take 15 minutes to quietly reflect and jot down your thoughts on the following:

1. How do you experience the Holy Spirit differently from God the Father and from Jesus Christ?
2. Does the Holy Spirit say to you: *"Do What Jesus Would Do?"* If not, what does the Holy Spirit say to you?

<u>Group Discussion/Share:</u>
Address the above questions one at a time and, for those who wish to share, discuss your answers/insights.

CHAPTER 8

BEING REJECTED

The High School Counselor had been quiet through most of this, then spoke up: *"Some of you guys know what I was going through with that Principal at the high school. I was hurting really badly, both from being told I was no good at what I was doing, not "gifted," and from the fact that the Principal had systematically selected which staff members to put on the chopping block. Anyway, I was at the same point as the Pastor was. I was a "basket case" in every sense of the word. I can remember thinking that everything I had ever learned about God and Christ was all mixed up and confused. I hit the wall. Slam!"*

The High School Counselor thought back to the group of High School employees who had asked for help from the Board of Directors of the high school and from Regional Council. He and the group of six other employees believed that the Principal was deceptive and a manipulator of the truth which was being fed to certain members of the Board. The Principal was smart. He would select strategic targets for his manipulation. Some were highly respected men and women in positions of leadership on the Board. These people, for unidentifiable reasons, were susceptible to being blinded to the truth. Maybe it was because they had been taught to hold the role of principal in reverence and high esteem, no matter what. In respect for the role, the Principal could only be right, never wrong. The Principal was the man chosen by God to lead them. To not respect him was to not respect God. What could be simpler?

The test of loyalty was simple. Did you support and cherish the Principal? If not, you were considered an enemy of the school. The Principal and his followers then commenced an orchestrated campaign of spreading rumors about any staff member or board member who did not pledge their alliance to the Principal. Secret meetings took place, where rumors and gossip were given birth. He remembered how the school's staff members had written individual statements to the Regional Council about the Principal, and had even asked to be interviewed by the Council's representatives.

The High School Counselor remembered how his written statements to the Council had been so clear in describing the emotional illness of the pastor.

"The spiritual life of the school is endangered because the Principal has created divisions between himself and his staff, himself and the Board Members, and to some degree the Board members and the staff. These divisions with staff have been created by:

- *refusing to trust his staff with his vision and goals,*
- *creating distrust within the staff regarding his ability to lead,*
- *making it very clear, early on in his position, that he would have preferred not to work with the present staff,*
- *his preference for talking negatively about staff members to other staff members,*
- *working with staff one-on-one rather than working as a team,*
- *manipulating the situation to either imply, or directly state, that a staff member is not thinking clearly or that their perception is incorrect."*

The result of this is that the Principal exonerates himself from any fault, the staff member is frustrated and is made to feel that what they experienced is of no consequence."

The newly hired Administrative Secretary wrote:

"I had decided to resign at the end of my first two weeks because I felt that the Principal's demeanor toward me was at many times condescending, rude, and disrespectful. I would also consistently feel confused about his requests because he would say one thing and then forget what he'd said, or change his mind and then implicate me as the problem for the confusion. I have seen him in deep depression one minute and then the next minute demonstrate a great show of affection toward a board member. I have heard him say with much enthusiasm and hugs, 'I love you! I love you!' Then, an instant later, he would slip back into his depressed mode. I have seen enough of this behavior to feel his character is very disingenuous.

I also feel that the Principal has continually been testing me for confidentiality in my position. For example, he would say, 'Kate is the only one I can trust; she's really earned my trust.' I felt that he was saying that he could trust her and not me. That he expected me to earn his trust to be seen by him as trustworthy."

Despite all this honest and objective reporting, the High School's Chairman of the Personnel Committee consistently stated, *"I will back the Principal all the way. That's the only way."* The High School Counselor and the others watched helplessly as the Regional Council took their findings about the emotional well-being of the Principal to the Board of Directors, only to be told to: *"stay out of our school."*

Generally, the Council agreed that there were serious problems, both with the emotional illness of the Principal, and with the serious divisions taking place in the school and with the Board. The factioning of the Board into several "war camps" was becoming quite evident, but the control exerted by the Principal over several of the powerful members of the Board was seemingly overwhelming.

Pulling himself out of these thoughts, the High School Counselor spoke up: *"Well, basically I have no choice since nothing else is working. So I will give control of my life to the Holy Spirit and pray 'Holy Spirit take it all, take my life, my career, my gifts, my weaknesses and do with me what you wish. I give you my hopes and dreams. I renounce my own agenda, my desires for personal recognition and reward, my personal financial goals, and my control over my life. Instead, I am resigned to Do What Jesus Would Do!'"*

In the silence that followed, the Pastor spoke up: *"I agree! I too will give up control of everything that is anything of mine to the Holy Spirit along with a desperate prayer that He will release me from my fears and anxieties."*

Study Guide – Chapter 8:
Being Rejected

Individual Reflection:

Take 15 minutes to quietly reflect and jot down your thoughts on the following:

1. Have you ever reached out to someone in authority for help only to receive no assistance? If yes, briefly describe one such experience.
2. How did you feel? In what ways were your confidence and/or self-worth impacted?
3. What were your thoughts/feelings, if any, about how God the Father became involved during this experience, if at all?
4. What were your thoughts/feelings, if any, about how Jesus Christ became involved during this experience, if at all?
5. What were your thoughts/feelings, if any, about how the Holy Spirit became involved during this experience, if at all?

Group Discussion/Share:

Address the above questions one at a time and, for those who wish to share, discuss your answers/insights.

CHAPTER 9

GIVING UP CONTROL

The Pastor continued: *"My question now is, 'What should we each do with this truth?' Why don't we agree that for the next couple of days, before we do anything, or decide anything, we ask ourselves 'have I given up control?'"*

There was grumbling in the air. A few of the men thought: *"Easy for you to say. I have spent my whole life trying to be the master of my fate: to raise a family, to create a business or career, to play by the rules, to save money for a rainy day. Now, all of a sudden, I'm supposed to stand down and give up control? How about my children? Am I supposed to say 'Sure kids, I don't have control, go ahead and do what you feel like doing?' And how about my job? When someone is trying to screw me, what do I say 'Go ahead and screw me?' If I don't have control, is it all in the hands of God? I don't think so!"*

The Pastor sensed the mood and responded: *"Guys you have got to give it up. You think you can control illness, all it takes is one cell to start to metastasize and you have cancer on your hands? You think you can control the randomness of when companies merge or when they go out of business, but it happens and you are out of a job. How about your kids? Do you think you can actually control who they marry or what choices they make? How about the aging process? You don't actually think you aren't going to get old and start to fall apart just like everyone else?*

We all have the illusion of control because while we are young we believe we control a lot of what goes on around us. But as we move through this world of ours, the list of things that we can't control gets longer and longer each year. So it is not if you will lose control, because unless you've got rocks in your head you know it is going to happen whether you like it or not. So fellas, instead of waiting to lose it, we have to give it up!"

By the way, when you "give it up," then the new problem is what to put in its place. That's where the Holy Spirit comes in. So the question to ask yourself is: 'Have I given up my sense of control about my life and have I asked the Holy Spirit to release me from my fears and anxieties about what I am now facing?'

Jesus taught us what to do, so we have a guide, an example and a beacon. In the Garden of Gethsemane he prayed, 'not my will but your will.' We must follow Jesus' example and overcome our inborn sense of fear and anxiety about giving up control. Until we do, we will be mired in a never ending circle of fear, selfishness, and anger. When we give up control we can invite the Holy Spirit to take its place and with the Holy Spirit guiding us, we can live the life that Jesus wants us to live. We can 'Do What Jesus Would Do!...Anybody not get this?"

The Pastor continued: *"The decision is not an easy one, and needs to be consciously made every day, every hour, every minute, in every decision before you, and in every circumstance with your family or at work. You have got to grapple with the distractions that are before you and make that decision. That's where prayer fits in. It is where we ask the Holy Spirit to help us.*

Sure, the distractions are enormous: money, power, influence, just plain busyness, physical fitness, children, spouses, the list goes on and on. The bottom line is that the Holy Spirit can counsel us to focus in on what is truly important.

Do What Jesus Would Do!...Anybody not getting this?"

Study Guide – Chapter 9:
Giving Up Control

Individual Reflection:

Take 15 minutes to quietly reflect and jot down your thoughts on the following:

1. How do you agree/disagree with the Pastor about the need to give up control?
2. How do you currently give up control?
3. When you do give up control, are you good at it? If yes, what helps you let go? If no, what gets in the way?
4. How often are you consciously aware of your decision to give up control and/or take control?
5. When you give up control of a situation, how might DWJWD fill the void?

Group Discussion/Share:

Address the above questions one at a time and, for those who wish to share, discuss your answers/insights.

CHAPTER 10

THREE YEARS LATER

What transpired in the lives of these six men was really remarkable.

the High School Counselor

The High School Counselor ultimately resigned from the Harvest Christian High School and said goodbye to the Principal and his illness, gave up his plans to obtain his Ph.D., and wholeheartedly launched his new career as a Youth Minister at a nearby church.

the Lawyer

The Lawyer closed his law practice and took a job at a large, well respected University. He created a major community event to bring "the Spirit" to children in the form of a 3K, 5k, and 10K *Run for Life*. The motto was: *"Celebrating the Spirit of Goodness in Children."*

the Pastor

The Pastor opened the Sonshine Kids Christian Day Care Center, although some said it could never be done. In his words: *"I gave everything that was anything of mine to the Holy Spirit with a desperate prayer that He would release me from my fears and anxieties. I turned into a totally different person. I no longer focused my sermons on keeping the 'establishment' happy, but I focused on what the Spirit was guiding me to say. I rejoiced at being able to teach about the great things that were possible in this church. We were becoming evangelical just as Jesus wanted us to be. And I could see us pulling together and giving up our individual agendas. And sure enough, things started to change. New people kept coming, lots of people from all different age groups, who wanted to be part of a relationship with Jesus, God the Father, and the Holy Spirit.*

Some of the 'establishment' did not want to be part of the change. I hated to see it happen, but some people left the church because things were changing. They did not want to lose their positions of 'power and influence,' so they left. This didn't bother me as much anymore. I realized I could love Jesus, and still care for those who needed love. The Men's Saturday Morning study got so strong that I no longer met with them. We started this Sunday morning group. We are starting a Women's Bible Group, and our Wednesday Night Family Dinners are really a great time. I remind myself as often as possible throughout the day to 'Do What Jesus Would Do!'"

the Electronics Guy

The Electronics Guy became seriously ill some time later and was hospitalized for an extended period. It was during his hospitalization that he remembered the conversation of that morning. It was only then that he understood and believed in the need to give up control of his life, and his guilt, to the Holy Spirit. When he recuperated he launched a new career, which was a new source of hope and optimism.

the International Banker

The Banker and his wife went with their son to the National Eye Institute in Bethesda.

the Retired Salesman

The Retired Salesman realized that just praying to Jesus and God the Father wasn't enough. He came to believe deeply that a 100% decision to release himself to the Holy Spirit was something he needed to do. He came to understand that the hand of God does not cause pain or hurt in life and that he needed the Holy Spirit to help him give up the anger he had carried for these many years about the death of his first wife.

During these years, when the "Bible Boys" saw each other around, their first or last words to each other were *"Do What Jesus Would Do!"*

But each story did not end there, and there was plenty of pain to come.

Study Guide – Chapter 10:
Three Years Later

Individual Reflection:

Take 15 minutes to quietly reflect and jot down your thoughts on the following:

1. Which of the men's stories, if any, do you most relate to? Why?
2. Looking back, how has the Holy Spirit get been involved in your story, if at all?

Group Discussion/Share:

Address the above questions one at a time and, for those who wish to share, discuss your answers/insights.

CHAPTER 11

THREE YEARS LATER –
THE DETAILS –
THE HIGH SCHOOL
COUNSELOR'S STORY

The High School Counselor continued to be in the middle of the crises caused by the Principal at the Harvest Christian High School. He initially watched his co-workers under attack, saw one after the other cave-in due to the fear and pressure, and ultimately experienced being attacked himself when the Principal targeted him. He watched as the other eight staff members held firm to the truth, and sought help.

Some couldn't withstand the pressure. The school's financial secretary, a young Mother with three children who was initially the strongest and angriest with the Principal, eventually broke. She had written to the Board Members within the first 4 months of the Principal's arrival:

"I feel that asking an employee to put a school related expense on their personal credit card, as I have been asked to do by the Principal on three separate occasions, is not procedurally correct and should be 'nipped in the bud' immediately."

Months later, after she had been subject to the Principal's attacks, after rumors and criticisms orchestrated by the Principal were lobbed against her, this same financial secretary decided that as a single mother she needed the job, and that she would not join with the other eight employees in making further statements to the Board or the Regional Council. She was simply afraid of losing her job.

The High School Counselor's friend, Kate, the Director of High School Center, wrote to the Regional Council the same things that she had written months before to the Board of Directors at the school:

"Soon after the Principal arrived, my feeling of excitement became a feeling of being frightened about the working conditions and my job security."

From her notes taken at meeting and during conversations, she provided quotes of statements made by the principal.

- *"If I leave that means that Satan has taken over."*
- *"I can't divulge what I heard, or who I heard it from."*
- *"You're paranoid."*
- *"You've been abused."*
- *"Look, she is going to cry."*
- *"I risked my neck for you."*
- *"The staff is unhealthy."*
- *"The staff is dysfunctional."*
- *"The staff is incompetent."*

- *"The staff is disloyal."*
- *"I should see results from your counseling."*
- *"I have low grade depression all the time, there, the secret's out."*
- *"I feel cut off at the knees."*
- *"I've giving up relating to the staff"*
- *"I feel lonely and alone."*
- *"I'm swimming and sinking."*
- *"I have no one to lean on."*
- *"I feel rocks are being thrown at me."*

The Principal's mood swings became very obvious. His expressions changed almost instantaneously from gregarious, friendly, the "life of the party," truly effervescent and ebullient, to those of somber darkness, unsure of himself, as if he were lost and in near panic, very introspective, and recessive. His eyes would darken with deep circles as if he were exhausted. It appeared to the staff that the effervescent personality did not know or remember what the recessive personality had done or said. It was like two persons in one.

Ultimately the High School Counselor became the prime target of the Principal. During the course of the year, the Counselor noted discrepancies between the Principal's words and deeds. He noted his threats to *"clear out the staff."* He heard the Principal deny statements that the Principal had plainly spoken. The Principal asked for the High School Counselor's help in evaluating the other staff members, and sought the Counselor's help in creating a situation that would force another staff member to leave. The Principal spoke to the Counselor of the Principal's perceptions of the staff's maturity, competency and character, occasionally blaming them for the Principal's difficulties. He continued to inquire into the details of their divorces and relationships and used what he learned against them.

Eventually, the Regional Council did assign two qualified, open minded and fair professionals: a psychologist and a senior business executive, to conduct an investigation. These two men interviewed all nine staff members. The interviews were free discussions of all the points raised in the staffs' statements.

The Regional Council then brought the results of their process to the Board of Directors of the Harvest Christian High School. Their reception was quite shocking. Rather than welcome the Council representatives, who were there to protect the school, a "fortress mentality" of the Principal's followers kicked into gear.

> *"The Council has no right coming into our school and telling us what to do. We love the Principal and we are devoted to him. It is just a few malcontents on staff that are all causing the problems."*

What was most remarkable, was that even during this increased scrutiny of the Principal, his behavior did not correct itself. Rather his emotional state exacerbated the situation because, with increasing frequency, he was unable to control himself. In some cases, the blind worship of the Principal by the "insider group" even emboldened him to his resolve, whether based in aberration or fact.

Kate, the Director of the Center, was asked to document what happened to her during an interview with the Principal and the Head of Personnel. Kate wrote:

> *"This is a written account of a meeting that took place this morning at approximately 9:40 a.m. I feel it is important to convey this information in regard to my being a witness for the ongoing investigation of the Principal by the Regional Council.*
>
> *The Principal called me into his office to meet with himself and the Chairman of the Personnel Committee. They were both dismayed with me about my 'speaking to the Regional Council' about the disenchantment of my*

working relationship with the Principal. The Personnel Chairman asked me if I had a copy of my statement. I answered 'at home.' He then asked me if I would share with them the contents of that statement. I responded, 'Under the rules of confidentiality, which I have read, I am not authorized to discuss this matter with any members of the school staff.' They then continued to encourage me to share information. I repeated this same statement several more times during this period of inquest.

They asked me who had encouraged me to make a statement. I responded 'Nobody…I did this of my own accord and for God.' The Principal then made it clear that he did not feel that we could continue working together. He asked me if I agreed. I responded, 'I enjoy my job and am capable of performing my responsibilities.' He added that 'You have betrayed me and I cannot trust you anymore.' To which I responded, 'I have done nothing wrong.' *He then said 'How can I continue to work with you when you have gone behind my back like this?' I repeated, 'I have done nothing wrong'. He then said, do you think you have the right to ruin this school?' I responded, 'I've only spoken the truth, I haven't ruined anything.' They then tried again to encourage me to share the contents of my statements to the Regional Council and I repeated my 'rules of confidentiality' statement.*

The Principal repeated that he could not continue to work with me under the circumstances, and asked if I agreed that this was a fair statement? I responded, 'I can't speak for you.' He then asked me how I would feel in 'his shoes.' I repeated that I couldn't speak for him.

The Personnel Chairman asked how I could continue working here under the circumstances. I responded that I would continue to fulfill my responsibilities as instructed. The Principal asked 'who instructed you on this?' I felt he was trying to find out who might have been counseling me. I again said, 'I will continue to fulfill my responsibilities as instructed when I was hired.'

He then repeated that he didn't see how we could continue working together. I looked at the Personnel Chairman and asked, 'So what does this mean?' He replied, 'Well, under the circumstances, we don't see any alternative but to ask you to submit your resignation.' I responded, 'No, I don't want to do that!' He said, 'We think it would be the best thing for the school.' I replied, 'No, I won't do that! The best thing for the school is the truth.'

The Principal jumped in and said, 'Well then we will have to terminate your employment.' I responded, 'It is unlawful to fire me simply because I have told the truth.' The Principal said, 'you are a Christian; do you think it is Christian to file a lawsuit?' I responded, 'I don't think I should comment any further.' He then said, 'Well, then we will decide for you and deal with a lawsuit if that is what you want to do. You can no longer work here.' I looked at the Personnel Chairman and asked him what this meant (wanting clarity in no uncertain terms). He agreed with the Principal and said that I was terminated and added, 'I am disappointed in you as a woman.' I responded, 'Mister Chairman, you don't know me very well and you're entitled to your opinion; am I free to go? He replied, 'Yes.'

As I stood up and took my first step, the Principal kept his right leg crossed to block my passage and said. 'No, let's wait a minute.' I sat down again, and he proceeded to talk with the Personnel Chairman, 'Perhaps we should go through the proper process for this. We'll bring this forward for the committee's approval and then take action. It is obvious; however, that we cannot continue working together.'

The Chairman agreed to the Principal's suggestion and said to me, 'understand that we expect that you will continue to work in a professional manner until we bring this forward to the committee.' I responded, 'Of course.' He then said that he wanted me to understand that 'my intention is to recommend to the Board next week that you be terminated.'"

The next day, the Chairman of the Personnel Committee handed her an article related to loyalty to leaders and said *"I've got something here that may be of help to you."*

The next day, she was summarily fired. She was called into the Principal's office at 9:15 a.m. and told that there had been a "special"

Personnel Committee meeting the night before, and *"we have a check for you covering you through today."* You are *"free to leave whenever you'd like,"* and if you'd like some help with your things, *"we've got some boxes here for you."*

Other school staff included the office secretary who had worked for five years at the school, as well as her successor, had also recently resigned. The talented and gifted young Music Director had resigned shortly before.

The High School Counselor was feeling like he was one of the last of the innocent ones. He and his friend the Lawyer, discussed the situation frequently. They could not fully comprehend that in the face of such obvious illness that people could have so misplaced their allegiance to the Principal. How could these Board Members permit such aberrant and illegal behavior to take place under their authority? Wasn't this supposed to be a Christian school where the love and rule of God were to be followed? Could people be so blinded that they would look to their leaders to receive the direction they felt was missing in their lives, even when these leaders were so obviously flawed? How could they become so confused that they would lose themselves? Are certain people particularly vulnerable to this form of "cult existence," where the devotion to an individual is so intense that they will allow themselves to be dulled and blinded to the truth? Why couldn't they look to the power that is within themselves? Why couldn't they feel the richness and calmness of the goodness of the Spirit?

In the end, the High School Counselor submitted his resignation and returned to his former church as a youth pastor. During all of this craziness, what kept coming back to him was: DWJWD. *"Do What Jesus Would Do!"*

In total all eight employees had left, yet the cliques of loyalists to the Principal remained. Eventually, the Board offered a six-figure settlement package to the Principal for the "treatment" he endured. The Principal then went off to a new school in Arizona.

Study Guide – Chapter 11:
Three Years Later – The Details - the High School Counselor's Story

Individual Reflection:

Take 15 minutes to quietly reflect and jot down your thoughts on the following:

1. Have you ever been fired, forced to resign a job, or laid off? If yes, briefly describe one such experience.
2. How was your confidence and/or self-worth affected?
3. What were your thoughts/feelings, if any, about how God the Father became involved during this experience, if at all?
4. What were your thoughts/feelings, if any, about how Jesus Christ became involved during this experience, if at all?
5. What were your thoughts/feelings, if any, about how the Holy Spirit became involved during this experience, if at all?

Group Discussion/Share:

Address the above questions one at a time and, for those who wish to share, discuss your answers/insights.

CHAPTER 12

THREE YEAR'S LATER –

THE DETAILS –

THE LAWYER'S STORY

The fear stopped. From that one morning with the "Bible Boys," it all stopped. By focusing on the Spirit of God within himself, the worry, anxiety, frustration, lack of concentration, even the persistent and unfamiliar reactions and pain of his body to the stress, all stopped. *"Do What Jesus Would Do!"*

He and his wife accepted an invitation to stay a weekend at their friends' cabin in the High Sierras. Their friends could tell that the couple was hurting and needed a place to retreat. With time to look back, to reengage with the Spirit who had been buried for several years, and to make some decisions, they went for a walk in the mountains.

The number of items on their agenda seemed overwhelming: where to live, where to go to church, where to work, the children, the family back East, even continuing membership in his service club, all weighed heavily on him. But it was a beautiful day, clear and cold. Fall was in the air, so the leaves were bursting with red and brown and yellow as the two started out.

Kate had been treated so very badly at the Principal's High School she was hurting all over. But she "was a survivor" as she would say frequently, and she was "up for any new adventure" that might come along. She had been a devoted mother, and it always surprised him that she seemed so ready to go back to the East Coast. She said she would handle it with air travel, phones, etc., but he always doubted her. She loved her family so deeply, and her children were such a part of her life. He feared moving away would ultimately catch up with her; at least that's what he thought to himself.

He had started floating resumes to family members back East. He was a licensed California attorney, so moving back East meant that he would not be licensed there as an attorney. The idea of being three thousand miles away from the children ultimately didn't sit well with him either. He and Kate loved their children and to be close enough for even semi regular visits with them was a part of that love and could not be risked. As they walked, he concentrated on giving up control of the situation. *"Do What Jesus Would Do!"*

So in those first quiet moments of the walk, they decided to stay in California.

The next item was the church. Now that she was no longer at the Principal's school, the option presented itself to seek out a new spiritual home or to continue at Harvest Christian, but only as a member of the congregation rather than a paid staff member. Unfortunately, the atmosphere at Harvest Christian, had turned caustic. The Principal had poisoned the community, and the Principal's clique remained to stoke the hate. Kate became the subject of cold-shouldering even from old friends. She was greeted by many with furtive glances that would immediately go down towards the floor. The rumors and false stories continued to swirl, even after the Principal was gone.

There was a large group of "refugees" from the Principal's school that had migrated over to the Community Church across town. Kate's old friend, the Pastor, was there. *"Do What Jesus Would Do!"* she thought.

In those quite moments, they decided together on a new church, the Community Church, and it was there he joined the "Bible Boys."

Next came the topic of the job. He knew that he was a good lawyer, half-surprising himself with his significant victory over four lawyers from one of the top Silicon Valley firms, but it left him financially broken. The reality of his financial problems was so difficult to believe. As they walked, he again gave his fear and disbelief over to the Holy Spirit, and he tried to reach a point of quiet within himself. *"Do What Jesus Would Do!"* he thought.

He had recently floated a resume to a large and well respected University. He quietly proposed to Kate that if he were offered a job, he would take it. The calmness of the moment surprised him. Kate, once again, gently supported the decision. Regardless, he would close his law practice. Holding on to the control of having his own business, no longer seemed all that important anymore.

Then came his service club. He had been a member for almost 18 years and the club had played a large role in his life. He and Kate had been to International Conventions in Australia, China, France, Canada and Scotland. They had started a program together eight years ago called *"Life Clubs"* in which local service clubs would "adopt" a local group of children. This was a dream and a passion for the couple for the past eight years. From their initial idea, they counted now over fifty countries that had at least one *"Life Club."* To quit his service club now would be horrid.

Many people, he thought to himself in the quietness of the moment, do not understand having a deep commitment to a service club. They see the social activities and parties, all the silliness of hats and badges, and dismiss the seriousness of the meetings. The truth is that more caring and good deeds, more significant acts of generosity, more concerted action for world peace and understanding, not to mention huge programs for children and young people, all come from international service clubs. Why people ever look down their noses at service clubs was a mystery to him. The passion and dedication of millions of members working so hard in all the service clubs around the world was testimony to the Spirit of Goodness in human beings. In many cases, the members gave of themselves unselfishly to tap into the enormous power for goodness in the world.

As they walked along on that fall day in the mountains, he thought about both the monetary and the time commitment that goes along with service club membership. Again he gave up the moment to the Spirit of God, and prayed to find what Jesus would have wanted him to do. He prayed: *"Oh Spirit help me have the courage and wisdom to find the correct path. Let me listen, be still and listen. Do What Jesus Would Do!"* he thought. Then insight struck him.

If the University job panned out, why not join the local service club by the university and continue in the international organization? *"My gosh, why not?"* The answer seemed so simple. He wondered to himself, why he had labored so painfully over this problem for so long? Clearly there had to be University staff members who belonged to the local chapter of the international service club. The eight years that he and Kate had put into *"Life Clubs"* could continue. *"Thank you dear lord for helping me to be open to the Spirit of God that is right here with us as we walk along. Thank you! Thank you!"* he prayed.

Next came the subject of the *"Run for Life."* and this would be the toughest decision of them all. For about a year, he had envisioned a major event which would take all of the regional *"Life Clubs,"* and draw the children and young people into a 3K/5k/10k walk/run, followed by a festival called the *"Celebration of Life."* He had identified a few sponsors, the course was still a problem, but he felt it could be pulled together.

As he and Kate walked along a quiet and contemplative mood surrounded them. An idea hit: Why not have a *"Spirit Service"* as the centerpiece of the day of activities? It could have a children's chorus for the vocals and musical accompaniment, and four or five spiritual leaders from several different churches speaking to the children and young people about the Spirit that is within each one of them.

But, he said to himself, as he had so many times before, *"Why do I have to be the one to do this? I've have got to have rocks in my head to try to organize a day long series of events, involving potentially thousands of runners and thousands of children, as well as police, ambulances, entertainment, not to mention city permits upon permits, and insurance!"* It means risking failure if the whole thing does not come together. It means asking people for money, for time, for advertising, for labor. Again he thought. *"Why does it have to be me to lead all this?"* And the answer came to him, *"Do What Jesus Would Do!"*

He was fording into areas of religion and faith he knew that he was not qualified to tread. He knew the words "religion" and "church" had negative connotations to many, many people. During the *"Spirit Service,"* he imagined there could be a lot of "turf battles" amongst the religions involved. A theme would be needed to help unite everyone.

The theme would need to be pleasing to God as well as to the many different religions that would be participating. A theme that would touch Christians, Muslims, Protestants, Jews, Catholics, believers as well as non-believers, as well as those of varying ethnicities and cultural heritages. A theme that would not offend the municipalities and the principle of "separation between church and state."

He prayed, *"Oh Holy Spirit is there such a unifying theme or message to breach all the chasms erected to separate us?"*

It was not during that walk in the mountains that a theme came, nor did it come like a bolt of lightning or a crack of thunder. It came rather slowly, over time, from calmness and an openness to the Spirit. It came from focusing on Christ and considering what He would want embraced. It came from regular prayer to the Holy Spirit to help free him from all of his prejudices, stereotypes, and fears of unknown people and religions. It came from resting and releasing to the Holy Spirit. It came from discernment and a process of eliminating the themes that did not capture the Spirit of God.

The theme that ultimately emerged: *"To celebrate the Spirit of Goodness in Children"*

It was simple, understandable, and inclusive. The word *"Spirit"* is capitalized to indicate the spirit being referred to is the Holy Spirit of God. The phrase "in children" emphasizes that each child carries within them the Spirit of God. With the theme in place, the goal became clearer and clearer: to convince children they have the Spirit of goodness within them and to teach them that they are loved and can love.

"It takes a village to raise a child." he supposed, and there are so many children who do not have a loving family or other adult or positive role model. He thought how the youth violence of today is mind numbing. The high school shootings demonstrate that certain children do not have any spiritual side to their lives. Yes, he thought, this is what Jesus would do – teach children that they are intrinsically good and that they carry that goodness within themselves wherever they go.

And when children get older, they can learn of the Holy Spirit and the power of the Spirit just like the "Bible Boys" had learned it. *"Do What Jesus Would Do!"* Yes. He would do this, even if it was painful, even it were exhausting, even it if would subject him to possible failure and embarrassment. He prayed: *"Holy Spirit, please help me find the peace, calmness, and perseverance to see the project through."*

In sharing these thoughts with Kate, he saw a path to their future, and he suddenly felt lighter. The details were not clear, but calmness seemed to invade the moment, as well as a happiness and contentment.

Well, the *"Run for Life"* took place the following April. The 3k, 5k and 10K walk/run started with a reception which included: members of the Shriners, Lions, Elks, Soroptimists, Scouts, representative from the local professional football team, along with local elected officials and community leaders.

Directly after the running awards were presented, the *"Spirit Service"* took place with 80 voices from the County Children's Chorus and five thoughtful, inspiring talks by: a Methodist Minister, a Roman Catholic Sister, a Presbyterian Pastor, a representative from the Jewish faith, and a non-denominational Christian Minister.

The event culminated with a *"Celebration of Life"* with food and game booths, a silent auction, and a full silver saddle equestrian show by the Shriners. The theme for the day, *"Celebrating the Spirit of Goodness in Children,"* was on every tee shirt, button, video and flyer.

Yet even in the face of such a successful event, there was criticism and contention from the regional service club leadership. It was an age old issue: one relating to money and control. The Regional Leadership Chairman formed a "Special Committee." He selected individuals, several of whom had no experience with the *"Life Club"* program or the *"Run for Life"* and intentionally excluded several individuals who had supported and had attended both. An evening meeting was called for the new "Special Committee" and the Lawyer was asked to attend. There was intentionally no agenda. He was walking into a set up.

In short, with the "decks stacked," he was asked to resign the Presidency of the *"Run for Life"* organization. The reasons given were not clear, but the dominant undercurrent was that regional leadership wanted to kill the *"Run for Life"* organization because it was seen as a competitive organization; one not under the Regional Service Club leadership's control. They did not want a "competitive organization" even if its purpose was the betterment of children. The easiest way for the Regional Service Club's leadership to gain control was to arrange for the forced resignation of the Lawyer, and that is what they did.

The Lawyer agreed to resign. Throughout the process he thought, *"Do What Jesus Would Do!"*

Study Guide – Chapter 12:
Three Year's Later – The Details – the Lawyer's Story

Individual Reflection:

Take 15 minutes to quietly reflect and jot down your thoughts on the following:

1. Do you use your highest skills in putting your faith into service to others? If yes – how? If no – why not?
2. If you serve others, why do you serve?
3. If you serve others, how do you decide how you will serve?
4. Have you found your service sweet spot or are you currently out of balance? Perhaps you serve in a way that stretches you too thin or in a way that does not push you far enough outside your comfort zone. If you haven't found your "sweet spot," what are you being called to do?
5. What role might the Holy Spirit play as you decide how to serve others?

Group Discussion/Share:

Address the above questions one at a time and, for those who wish to share, discuss your answers/insights.

CHAPTER 13

THREE YEARS LATER –
THE DETAILS –
THE PASTOR'S STORY

The reality of the times refused to dissipate at the Community Church, and the 44-year-old Pastor continued to be in the cross hairs. He was a "baby boomer" and was very gifted in so many talents. His sermons were stories woven with belly bending humor, a tenderness that comes from a kind soul and a special thoughtfulness, and were also gently challenging to the congregation to love God and care for those in need. Several believed that he was one of the most gifted teachers, speakers, and biblically sound orators that they had ever heard.

The Pastor was not without his weaknesses. The depression would creep in from time to time. He could be abrupt when he was caught off guard in responding to a question or comment. To some older members, for whom respect was of critical importance, feelings did get hurt, as the Pastor did not always give the "proper" respect and deference that the members of the "older generation" felt they deserved.

A pattern started to emerge, one which was becoming a demographic reality in just about every church, business, and governmental agency throughout the country. The "older generation" had the money and the "younger generation" was close to broke. The "older generation" had typically been with their companies for in excess of twenty years or more, had retirement accounts, and were in many respects enjoying their "golden years." The church experience was a major source of their feelings of self-worth. The experience of leadership was considered, by them, to be very important for their self-image. Their church was a place to feel that they were still relevant and important. They felt they should be heard and listened to by the "younger generation."

The "younger generation" had a very different financial profile. A job in excess of three years was considered somewhat unusual, college expenses for their children had quadrupled in ten years, mergers and acquisitions were making long term planning an impossibility, and the cutting and trimming in most businesses made expendable cash a nice thought, but not something to expect. The world had pushed into the new millennium with a whole new set of financial realities. In some states, public education had not kept up with the needs of the new wave of college students, and debt became the new norm. Generally, money was a problem for the "younger generation" in a way it no longer was for their older counterparts.

In a small church, the loss of one of the "older generations" could have a significant to devastating effect on the church's finances. A few deaths or sicknesses of several of the "older generation" could push the finances of a small church into semi-crisis mode. As these patterns were emerging, the prospects were not good. In the face of these trends, the Pastor stayed with his belief that a Christian day care center was a proper mission of the church. His heart would ache as he believed that the "older generation" was losing sight of the real calling of Jesus "to make disciples of all people." He was afraid that he would get lost in the fears of the "older generation." A generation that had lived through the Great Depression and one or both world wars, and who had a very different view of money.

There were; however, many that shared the Pastor's view and a welling up of support, action, volunteerism, and donated talents for the day care started to surface. As in every community, first came those who were the talented organizers and planners. They took leadership roles to ensure the old, large, dirty hall, formerly used by the commercial preschool, was turned it into a light, airy, multi-colored, clean, repainted, decorated, re-plumbed and rejuvenated place called the *"Sonshine Kids Christian Day Care."*

Saturday work parties were organized and everyone that could be out there, was: cutting and trimming trees, soundproofing the 40-foot high ceilings, cutting new windows, securing locks, cleaning, cleaning, and more cleaning. The "older generation" would work the gardens and the other "low to the ground" work. The "younger generation" was up on the roof, redoing the lighting, removing the eight 40 foot diseased pine trees from the parking lot, and tearing up the plumbing and the yard to comply with city codes. There is probably nothing more wonderful than when a pure volunteer effort, comprised of every sort of talent, is brought to bear on a God centered project.

During the same time, other volunteers were setting up the accounting records, interviewing and hiring a Day Care Director, and attending City Council meetings for all the many and varied permits required. All dissension was lost as the positive feelings and sense of accomplishment was collectively felt by all members of the church. All hurdles were overcome and the day of opening approached with great enthusiasm. The opening of the *"Sonshine Kids Christian Day Care"* seemed to bring a sense of new hope and a fresh beginning for all.

But as is human nature, once the initial intensity of joint accomplishments subsided old doubts started to resurface. While the day care was open, doing well on all counts with the prospects of achieving the school first year's goals on course, the Community Church started to slip into serious financial trouble. The income needed to sustain the Community Church was not there. There was a general recognition that the day care would ultimately bring in new young families, which would reestablish a firm financial base to the church, but the old fears and criticisms were proving to be true. There was not currently enough money for the church! And whose fault must that be?

Well of course, the 44 year old Pastor's! During this time of revival of the church and focus on the day care, the Pastor was happy in his ministry and with his relationship with God. He preached regularly on the Holy Spirit with all the thoughtfulness and skill and elegance that he had ever had. He lived *"Do What Jesus Would Do!"* every day. He was at peace with himself because he realized that he was not in control. He recognized in his personal walk with God, that he had given up his church to God. He prayed every day for the power to release his life to the Holy Spirit and *"Do What Jesus Would Do!"*

Now that a financial crisis was upon the Community Church, he could have slipped back into the old pattern of depression, anger at himself and his inability to resolve the situation, blame toward the church members for focusing on their own agendas, and frustration with God for allowing it all to happen, but instead he saw the positive. This financial crisis was occurring, yet things were gradually turning up at the *Sonshine Kids Day Care*. Occasionally he did feel the white hot blast of anger for being criticized unfairly, but he refused to give in to it. He told himself, *"Do What Jesus Would Do!"*

Ultimately he did not seek control over the church leaders, nor the problems, nor the human foibles. He held fast to his prayer: *"Oh*

God, let me release my anger and frustration. Let me listen to you oh Holy Spirit. Let me deny myself these feelings of frustration, anger, powerlessness, and negativism at the church leaders who want to have control and power."

He remained content and at peace even when the church leaders wanted to control the problem by reducing expenditures by removing him as Pastor. And that is what happened. After being unable to bring an easy remedy to the church's financial situation, the Elders, in private and without input from the congregation at large, asked him to leave. It was done behind closed doors.

Study Guide – Chapter 13:
Three Year's Later – The Details – the Pastor's Story

Individual Reflection:
Take 15 minutes to quietly reflect and jot down your thoughts on the following:

1. Have you experienced a situation and/or crises in your church which created division? If yes, briefly describe one such experience.
2. What were your thoughts/feelings, if any, about how the Holy Spirit became involved during this experience, if at all?

Group Discussion/Share:
Address the above questions one at a time and, for those who wish to share, discuss your answers/insights.

CHAPTER 14

THREE YEAR'S LATER –
THE DETAILS –
THE ELECTRONICS GUY'S STORY

After the "Bible Boys" that particular morning, The Electronics Guy's life had really not changed that much. He was well steeped in the Bible, he thought, and was confident that he had things figured out pretty well. He was a regular member of the "Bible Boys" and he sang in the "Proclaim" team, the elite singing group of the Community Church. The nine voices and instrumentation of the team were quite excellent. He loved to lift up his voice to praise God and he loved Jesus deeply.

Recently, he and his wife had become extremely excited about the prospect of joining one of the most popular multi-level marketing businesses in the country. Attending a multi-level marketing convention over a long weekend in Georgia or Texas was now something that energized their lives. When he returned from a convention, his enthusiasm for work was unrelenting. He was thrilled with the photos and marketing brochures showing how plain ordinary couples, with no advanced education or experience, could amass a fortune, along with houses, boats, motorcycles, and all with the freedom they desired.

Simultaneously, the Electronics Guy worked in a video rental store and for two small family owned businesses, picking up odd jobs and doing electronics. After the military, he had been in the video production business for several years, but he realized that type of lifestyle would cause him to be tempted into a fast life of drugs. He wanted no part of that.

In anger, he recently quit the video store job. Despite his best efforts, his anger still intermittently erupted out of control. Now his work focused on two family owned electronics businesses. The owners were like family, and he was "treated with respect," which was very important to him. He was Sicilian by God; and respect mattered! Most days, he had some freedom when he drove around the area to pick up or deliver a TV or DVD. He did not have any higher education and believed that his career options were few, except for the hopes and promises of his new "business."

Then one day, while lifting a 50-pound television, he felt as sharp hot cutting sensation in his lower intestines. He was rushed to the hospital and put under observation. After several days, the doctors could still not explain what was causing the pain. The absence of an explanation had a chilling effect, and he found himself confronting anger, frustration, medical incompetence (he thought), weakness, loss of appetite, weight loss, and muddling effects of heavy doses of pain killers and sedatives. He felt he was in a free fall. It was unbelievable that the doctors could not tell him what the problem was! What was to be a few days, turned into a week, then ten days, and there was still no definitive diagnosis. He could not keep any food down, so his diet consisted of ice, popsicles, and a tube inserted into his left hand.

Fear started to creep in. He was only 40, but what if he didn't make it? After 15 days in the hospital a realization swept over him; he was not in control of his life. He may not make it through this. He was losing weight, at a serious pace, and the doctors still could not explain what was causing it.

He thought about his life, what he had done with it. He felt anger at the people who had been the cause of all his problems. He felt depressed that it could be over before he did all the things he wanted to do, before he went all the places he wanted to go. He started to deal with his "real" belief in God and Jesus and realized that he might be leaving this world with a record that he wasn't too proud of. He became more afraid and felt more and more out of control.

At one of these moments, he tried to recall the phrase that he had kicked around with the "Bible Boys" that morning, over a year ago. What was it again?

Was it WWJD? *What Would Jesus Do?* No that was what was printed on the wristbands and stuff. That only asks the question; it doesn't do the do.

Was it WDJD? *What Did Jesus Do?* No, no that wasn't it! That sounds more like Bible study where you're learning about what Jesus did; there's more to it than that.

Was it DWJD? *Do What Jesus Did?* No, no that's a bit much! I sure can't do what Jesus did. I'm not God! I'm certainly not all powerful.

Was it DWJWD? *"Do What Jesus Would Do!"* That it! That's the call to action in today's world. That's the saying calling us to listen to what the Holy Spirit is telling us.

The best part, he thought, was the Holy Spirit is always with us, so I don't have to go out and find him. He is right here, right now, in this hospital room, in my spirit. He is the God who is my counselor and consoler, who only wants to help me breakaway from all my weaknesses. The God that wants to help me overcome my fears. The God that will help me live the life that Jesus wants me to live. But first

I must be willing to give up control. I must be willing to release my life, my dreams, my anger, my hurts, my frustrations, and my guilt to the Holy Spirit. *"Do What Jesus Would Do!"* he thought.

He began to pray, *"Holy Spirit free me from the anger, guilt, and hurt that I have inflicted on myself as well as my family. Take control of my life. Dear Holy Spirit, I release my life to you. I cannot control my outcome at this hospital, nor can I make this disease leave my body. I can though, give everything that I call mine over to you. Holy Spirit, through your power within me, I give you my whole being in the peace of God the Father, and in the name of Jesus the Son."*

At that moment, the fear ended. The freefall stopped.

Study Guide – Chapter 14:
Three Year's Later – The Details –
the Electronics Guy's Story

Individual Reflection:
Take 15 minutes to quietly reflect and jot down your thoughts on the following:

1. Do you think about your death? If yes, how often? If not, why not?
2. Have you ever consciously planned for your death? If yes, how?
3. If you were asked today, *"What did you do with your life?"* how would you respond?
4. As you think about your remaining time on this earth, how might the Holy Spirit be involved in expanding your answer to the question, *"What did you do with your life?"*

Group Discussion/Share:
Address the above questions one at a time and, for those who wish to share, discuss your answers/insights.

CHAPTER 15

Three Years Later –
the Details –
the International
Banker's Story

The Banker's story picks up at the trip to the National Eye Institute in Bethesda Maryland for his son's eye. During the two years that followed, the Banker and his wife lived a surreal existence. The horrific experience of Bethesda was hard to get over. The National Eye Institute, home to eight of the world's finest eye experts, diagnosed his son's condition in layman's terms as his retina being rejected by his own body. When this occurs, the body produces fluids around the eye which literally attack the retina; much like our own immune systems attacks an infection or bacteria.

The experts agreed that the primary objective was to save the boy's eye. So a remarkable, unbelievable and horrific procedure was planned to do just that. The 7 year old would undergo:

- a cataract surgery
- a total removal of the vitreous fluid in his eye, essentially all the "bad fluid"
- a cryogenic process to "freeze" the eye and seal up all the "normal" sources of the "bad fluid"
- insertion in the boy's eye of a gas bubble, for a 3 month period, to block or close any further creation of the "bad fluid"
- then, for one and a half months, he would have to lie face down, motionless, to allow the gas bubble to release an inert gas, which would be absorbed into the boy's eye
- the gas would then cause his body to begin to create brand new "good fluid"
- finally, if it all this worked, which was not guaranteed or even assured, his son's eye might have a chance; otherwise he would definitely lose his left eye and face the possible loss of his right eye; he could be blind by the age of eight!

It was during his treatment and ongoing therapy that he and his wife were "prayer warriors." They continued to tithe the full 10% to the Community Church and expected and waited for God to create a miracle for their son. To him, this plan sounded pretty reasonable.

During this time period, which stretched over two years, he remained deeply committed to the *Sonshine Kids Day Care Center*. In many ways, he became the "brains" of the group that comprised the Board of Directors. The financial undertaking to launch a day care center was not trivial by any means. There was a line of credit that had to be applied for and secured by the Council. Budgets had to be crunched with Excel spreadsheets, payroll services, taxes, and salaries for the day care director and staff of between 8 to 15 employees all took enormous amounts of time. There was also the time consumed by the challenges and problems facing any start-up business. The only volunteer who had the necessary financial and accounting skills, knowledge and experience, was the Banker. He did it all, and he did it with skill and generosity, while traveling on international business trips and worrying about his son and wife.

He was also the "heart" of the group. When asked about how he managed to handle everything, he would always say: *"Hey, I fake it till I can make it."* He would laugh and then, in his gentle and soft spoken manner, he would remind the Board, that *Sonshine Kids* was all about being Christian in all our dealings, whether they be with the children, parents, staff, and/or volunteers. When a parent would ask for a "scholarship" based on financial need, he would gently remind the Board members of the Christian values that the center should embrace. He would couch all requests in terms of whether they would bring a person closer to the Lord. If ever there was a couple deserving of a 100% full tilt miracle for their son, it was the International Banker and his wife.

The International Banker and the Lawyer planned to meet for a quick "catch-up" at the same coffee shop where the "Bible Boys" had met four years before. Over coffee, the Banker shared:

"The first year when our son was so sick, we became 'prayer warriors'; we tithed to the church and worked hard; yet nothing seemed to help our son. My wife got stronger in her faith during this time, but I have been sliding down into the valley and right now, I'm down in the depths. I started to get frustrated with the church, with myself, with God. At this point, I basically want to put God behind me. I just have no enthusiasm for the church anymore. I still love God in my heart, but I would rather just do other stuff. My wife has talked me into going to church again, but I just feel lost there. What is so remarkable to me is that while the church has been devastated from the Pastor leaving, and all its financial problems, the Sonshine Kids Day Care Center is thriving. Anyway,

our son now has 20/40 in his left eye, which is just about normal. He used to have 20/2000, which was basically blind. He wears an external contact and his eye has 'calmed.' We expect that we are over the worst of it now. He seems to be a normal little boy again. So I ask myself, 'Is this outcome the result of technology, the medical professionals, or was it God's grace?' I just don't know."

The international Banker sat back in his seat and slumped, as the realization set in from the telling of his story that he had never thought once about the Holy Spirit during the last several horrendous years of dealing with his son's eye.

There was a long silence before the Lawyer, seemingly coming to the same conclusion asked, *"I wonder why you did not pick up on the Holy Spirit through all of this?"*

The International Banker responded, *"You know, I don't think I could have seen the Holy Spirit if He was stuck right in front of my face."* Then he asked, *"Why do you put such emphasis on the Holy Spirit anyway? Isn't the Holy Spirit just the same as God?"*

The Lawyer answered, *"Look, my entire Bible study consisted of the sessions I had sitting right over there with you guys, so I don't know much of anything."* Both broke out in a good belly laugh, thinking about the rag-tag group of men collected at those "Bible Boys" sessions all those years ago. *"But when we talked about the Holy Spirit that day, it dawned on me that while I may not understand any of it, the simple truth is that the Holy Spirit is as powerful as God the Father, and Jesus Christ. It was Jesus who said 'Guys, I'm checking out of here and going back to God the Father, but don't panic! We are sending the Holy Spirit to be inside each of you, to guide you, until the end of time.'"*

"Now, I don't claim to understand how it all works, but you've got to admit, it sure sounds important! We have God the Holy Spirit as powerful as God the Father and God the Son sitting right here at this table with us right now!"

The International Banker added, *"You know, part of my problem is* that God the Father has always seemed real and sometimes, Jesus does too, but I tend to forget about the Holy Spirit all together."

Another pause grabbed the moment.

He continued, *"You know, my father-in-law is a minister and I asked him once what the Trinity was all about. He explained that he was a father-in-law to me; a father to my wife; and a husband to his spouse. He said that while he is one person, he relates totally differently to me, to his daughter, and to his wife. That's how he explained the Trinity to me, one God that has three different relationships."*

The Lawyer pondered a bit then said, *"You know, I don't think God had anything to do with your son's eye disease. The world we live in is so random. Think about DNA and the vast combinations of genes and chromosomes that make up each one of us. Think about the random plane that goes down, the drunk that runs the red light, the leader of a church, a service club, or a country who loses touch with reality. I don't think God preordains any of that."*

The International Banker replied, *"You might be right. This world is so random. Anything can happen to any of us. Maybe it's not about what happens to us, it's all about how we react to it. Maybe that's where the Holy Spirit comes in. I think this conversation could be my turning point. Thank you."*

The Lawyer: *"I'm glad to hear it! I suppose there's hope for us all if ordinary guys like us can stumble onto the fundamental truth that the Holy Spirit is so pervasive that He reaches into all aspects of human behavior and human relationships. If you're open to it, your relationship with the Spirit can be the cornerstone for getting through the loss of a job, financial hardship, sickness, the suffering of a child, the death of a spouse or any other deep pain that we all have to endure at certain times in our lives.*

With the Spirit, we can endure false or even emotionally ill leadership within the organizations we care about so deeply, whether they are a school, a church, a synagogue, a mosque, or a service club. Leaders in any organization can espouse caring slogans, but they are just other humans who are susceptible to the allure of power, control, and as always, money, just like everyone else.

With the Holy Spirit there is a way for us to get through each day with a sense of peace and contentment that is available for us to share with others if we become aware of it and ask for this grace. I think we are each called to take this truth and do something with it. To take on projects, challenges, opportunities, needs, and 'Do What Jesus Would Do!" The Spirit gives us the courage to be bold and to push ourselves to the limit of our skills and resources, because we are no longer held back by fear."

Study Guide – Chapter 15:
Three Years Later – The Details –
the International Banker's Story

Individual Reflection:
Take 15 minutes to quietly reflect and jot down your thoughts on the following:

1. In your own words, what is your understanding of the Trinity?
2. Do you believe you are asked to try and understand the Trinity? Why or why not?
3. Do you give equal attention to each of the three persons in one God? If yes, how? If no, why not?

Group Discussion/Share:
Address the above questions one at a time and, for those who wish to share, discuss your answers/insights.

CHAPTER 16

THREE YEARS LATER –
THE DETAILS –
THE RETIRED SALESMAN'S STORY

There is an old adage: "When you get old, you get really, really good, or you get really, really bad!" Well, the Retired Salesman and his wife clearly fell into the former category. At 80 years young, he had more things wrong with his body than most people had listed on their weekly grocery list. Because of this reality, he would often say with a glint in his eye: *"I never buy green bananas!"* Despite these ailments, he had an enthusiasm for his family and friends, his church and his God which seemed boundless. He was committed to the Jesus he loved; and to his woman who also loved Jesus with this same passion. They could be seen hobbling into and out of hospitals, doctor's offices, pharmacies, and treatment centers always with those same irascible smiles. They were in that phase of life where planning trips, and canceling trips, and planning and canceling all sorts of things were just part of the normal routine.

Then his wife, the light of his life, was diagnosed with cancer, and his old fears began to return. He'd lost his first wife years ago after ten debilitating years with Alzheimer's. He couldn't go through this again. He couldn't lose Gretchen too. In his prayers he cried out, *"Oh God, please do not do this again. She is a good woman and she should not suffer. Lord, I don't believe that I could withstand the loss of this women."*

In his quiet moments, he knew well his own weaknesses. He knew how despite his outward appearance of internal happiness and joy, it was this woman who was so much the cause for his joy. He could feel himself slipping into despair. If she were to become permanently disabled or die, he knew he would not have the power to control his own fall into bitterness.

"Do What Jesus Would Do!" he remembered from that coffee shop conversation those many years ago.

His history was not that much different than many of his generation. He was born in the mid-west and had kicked around town as a young man. He was not required to join the military, and he often found employment difficult. He ultimately settled into a sales position in the Midwest for a large chemical and agricultural supplier. Things seems pretty good, but the travel and moving from place to place into ever increasing levels of sales management, did not qualify for retirement benefits in any one company.

Back then California was exploding with opportunity, so he and his wife and their one daughter moved to the Golden State and settled down into the American dream. He purchased a beautiful home in a new emerging town, joined a local church, fostered friendships, and stayed with one company for many years. Over time, he became a wealthy man due in great part to the astronomical increase in the value of California real estate. Life was good. God was good. When he studied his Bible, or acted in his capacity as a Church Elder, he knew in the case of a problem he could pray and God would take care of it. He was convinced that God had a *"plan for each one of us."*

Since God was a *"good God"* and the world was his creation, and since he was a servant of this all powerful God, then success in life was strictly a function of his faith. Pretty simple.

Then Alzheimer's hit his first wife and he was shaken to his core. At first, prayer and faith were the obvious answers, so he devoted himself to that approach while at the same time finding the finest medical help available. One year dragged into three, then five, then seven, then nine, and after ten years of physical, emotional, and spiritual exhaustion, the journey came to an end. His wife died.

By this time, he was in bad, bad shape. He had booked a cruise for him and his wife to try to mark time in the long struggle against the disease. It was just before their time to leave when his wife quietly slipped into death. Friends of his knew that he was drained in every possible way, and they insisted that he, for the sake of his own life and health, take the cruise. The memorial services could wait for his return his friends insisted.

Well, he went on that cruise and was able for the first time in ten years to rest without heartache, anxiety, worry, or anger over the care of his wife weighing on his heart and mind. It was as if he had been dying himself day after day for those ten years. As he reflected, he realized he was conflicted about his old conviction that God was a good God and had a *"plan for each of our lives."* He had deep scars in his heart etched by ten years of pain. It was as if his heart had been hit by continuous droplets of water cutting into a great mountain, and over time deep fissures had been carved in his faith.

Time passed, and he could not seem to reconcile his experiences in life with his faith in the power of prayer and his belief in God's plan. He was vaguely conscious that he no longer fully believed the teachings of the Bible that God was the *"All Powerful,"* the *"Omnipotent One"* who has a plan for what was to happen in our lives. He wondered: *"Why would God allow what had happened to his beloved wife? How could such suffering have been God's plan?"* He found himself replaying the old Biblical phrases he had memorized and with the confidence of a salesman he proclaimed the power of God on earth, yet inside himself he deeply resented and felt angry with God in the deepest recesses of his heart.

Years passed, and then one day he met Gretchen. She was from Rhode Island, with a charming touch of a New England accent. She was widowed and had recently relocated to California to be closer to family. She too had acquired some wealth and was also deeply devoted and a committed believer in Jesus.

She had an interesting way of reciting the Lord's Prayer. After the words, *"Our Father Who art In Heaven,"* she would recite to herself, *"and within me."* She intensely believed in the God that was within her. Often she would find herself trailing others in the prayer because she wanted to remind herself each time she prayed that the Holy Spirit was within her. She prayed for the Spirit to be alive and active in her life.

She was just a joy to be around, an intelligent and natural leader who, over the years, had volunteered and led just about every form of church activity you could think of. She was perfect for him. Together they seemed like two snuggly kittens that nuzzled each other all the time and just loved every minute. Their personalities which shone alone brightly, were all the more radiant together. They sold their homes and decided to move into a smaller apartment to start their new life together. This is how they came to join the Community Church, and how he became one of the "Bible Boys."

So ultimately, as he sat there that morning with the rest of the "Boys," he was facing the knowledge of his beloved wife's newly discovered cancer. All those years of doubt, anger, resentment, and loss of faith in a "good God" came back upon him like an attacking animal. Hearing the discussion that morning about the Holy Spirit and giving up control pushed him to remain listening with an open mind and open heart.

Maybe the idea of a God who causes all things to happen in the world, was just plain wrong? Maybe God never preordains how a life is to be lived? Maybe the suffering of his first wife was not the handiwork of God? Maybe God had nothing to do with it? Maybe the way he prayed all these years wasn't right after all? *"Do What Jesus Would Do!"* he thought.

He began to think about his life in a whole new way. He no longer believed that all that happened to him or to his first wife was the act of God's hand. He realized, that despite his wife's cancer diagnosis or the bolts of pain that shot through his own body, what was important was not what life threw at him, but rather how he reacted. Would he respond with anger or resentment, or would he respond by giving up the control of his wife's illness and his own life to the Holy Spirit and asking for help in dealing with the difficulties? DWJWD became his motto.

Study Guide – Chapter 16:
Three Years Later – The Details – the Retired Salesman's Story

Individual Reflection:
Take 15 minutes to quietly reflect and jot down your thoughts on the following:

1. Have you ever dealt with a chronic medical condition, either your own or a loved ones?
2. When dealing with this, did you ever ask God "Why me?" If yes, what do you think was God's response?
3. Looking back, did the Holy Spirit become involved in any way? If so, how?
4. Did you ever become frustrated with God's response or lack of response?
5. When faced with this type of frustration, how might you consider DWJWD?

Group Discussion/Share:
Address the above questions one at a time and, for those who wish to share, discuss your answers/insights.

CHAPTER 17

Eight Years Later – All Six Men

the High School Counselor's Story

Out of the blue, a few of Harvest High's former staff were contacted by an Arizona school about the problems they were having with the Principal, who had relocated to Arizona after leaving the Harvest Community School. The Board Members of the Arizona school, through the assistance of the Arizona Regional Council, produced a report about the Principal which had been prepared by two consultants after receiving 167 surveys and conducting numerous interviews and found:

- *"Failure to maintain confidences"*
- *"Lack of leadership and ethics"*
- *"Lack of confidence, integrity, and trust"*
- *"Unilateral decision to dismiss the entire Administrative/Personnel Committee"*
- *"High degree of staff turnover and turmoil"*

- *"Environment of name calling, secret meetings"*
- *"Letter writing campaigns"*

There was great confusion about what was happening and why. The Arizona Board Members were being affected by letter writing campaigns, invitations (or lack thereof) to secret meetings, and rumors. The innuendos and gossip were growing to proportions which escalated into a high level of conflict and distrust.

The consultants interviewed even more members of the Arizona school and when even more scathing observations surfaced, the Principal was offered another six-figure settlement package and left the school in Arizona.

From what he went through with the Principal, the High School Counselor's life had been changed deeply and permanently. By looking to the Holy Spirit within himself, he found a clear vision to pursue a life of service to God by becoming a career Youth Minister. He found that all of his natural talents emerged again once he was in the presence of young people. His humor, his music, his sensitive and open feelings of respect for the young, all returned a hundred fold and the young men and women began to gravitate toward him and his way of thinking, praying, and living.

Now the High School Counselor, turned Youth Minister, is becoming a much sought after speaker. He speaks regularly at a major Christian summer youth camp and at seminars.

the Lawyer's Story

The Lawyer took a job at that well-respected University and joined the local chapter of the same international service club. He and his wife still promote their "Life Club" program at the international level.

The "Run for Life" and "Spirit Service" are again in active stages of planning and the University is even considering hosting the event, which now has the possibility to grow beyond the Lawyer's greatest expectations and touch the lives of thousands of children throughout the region. The theme of the event is: *"Celebrating the Spirit of Goodness in Children."* The Regional Leadership, that had demanded the resignation of the Lawyer, now believes they have the desired control. They never found a replacement for the Lawyer as president of the original non-profit corporation, so the non-profit has closed.

the Pastor's Story

Today, the Pastor is the senior pastor of a small church in the East. He continues to be happy and content with what happened at Community Church. The *Sonshine Kids Christian Day Care* is still thriving; enrollment is at a maximum, the teachers are bringing the message of God, Jesus and the Holy Spirit to the hearts and minds of the children who attend each day. The Community Church's financial crisis has not dissipated as attendance is at record lows. The Elders continue to believe that their control is essential. They are now looking for a pastor who will see things their way.

the Electronics Guy's Story

The Electronics Guy ended up having emergency surgery. The doctors removed a section of his large intestines which had developed a very unusual viral infection. By the time he left the hospital, he had lost close to 35 pounds, but he had changed in many more significant ways.

He was convinced, in the depth of his heart, that throughout his whole life he had been trying to control the people and things around him. He realized that when other people or things did not live up to his expectations, he would either get angry, "check out" through use of drugs, or simply walk away from something that was out of his control. He came to understand that as a human being, he would always be susceptible to these weaknesses, but he convinced himself that he could overcome these tendencies by looking to the Spirit of God within himself to help him release his need for control and to beg for God's help in his reaction to disappointing circumstances. *"Do What Jesus Would Do!"* became his new mantra.

From there, the rest of his life fell into place. He continued with his two jobs and was happy in the skills he had developed, the friends he had made, and with the customers who appreciated and respected his work. He moved forward with his multi-level marketing business, but with a new sense of calmness and a lack of anxiety. He knew that he and his wife were reasonably intelligent and resourceful and "the business" was just another way to support their family. The enthusiasm he felt was no longer directed at the houses, cars, boats, etc. It was directed at the sense of appreciation and thankfulness he felt for his wonderful wife and family, and for his place in the world as a member of the family of God.

the International Banker's Story

The conversation between the Lawyer and the International Banker did turn out to be his turning point. By the time the two men had walked out to the parking lot, the Banker was exuberant. *"It's all starting to make sense to me,"* he said. *"God and Jesus have always seemed far away, but the Holy Spirit is with us, with me, guiding me to 'Do What Jesus Would Do!'"* A wide and happy smile began to radiate from this newly energized man.

They shook hands, and each man was smiling broadly, with an incredible sense that something important had just happened, something very special, something very spiritual; yet something very unplanned and unexpected. As they went to their cars at opposite ends of the small parking lot, the Lawyer turned to wave and shouted across the parking lot: *"Do What Jesus Would Do!"*

The International Banker still serves as the Financial Officer of the *Sonshine Kids Day Care*. The center is at maximum capacity and is thriving! And, best of all, his son remains a heathy little boy!

the Retired Salesman's Story

The Retired Salesman and his loving wife are still going strong; still in love with their God and with each other. Their broad happy smiles inspire, and serve as role models to all. His total devotion to God the Father, Jesus Christ the Son, and his new understanding of the role of the Holy Spirit has made a profound impact on him. He no longer prays for an illness to go away or for the pain to be alleviated. His doctors are good enough for that. Now he prays, when either he or his loving wife must face these trials, that the Holy Spirit will help him to give up control of his human weaknesses, his doubts, his anger, and his resentments. He prays *"Do What Jesus Would Do!"* so that the Spirit will help him focus on the peace and joy to be found from the knowledge that God loves them, and also wants their pain and illnesses to be gone.

The "Bible Boys" never met much after that one eventful morning years earlier, but in their own way each never forgot *"Do What Jesus Would Do!"*

DWJWD!

Study Guide – Chapter 17:
Eight Years Later – All Six Men

Individual Reflection:
Take 15 minutes to quietly reflect and jot down your thoughts on the following:

1. If you take away one thing from these stories what would it be? DWJWD?
2. Does *"Do What Jesus Would Do!"* make sense to you? Why? Why not?
3. How has your understanding, feelings, and/or thoughts about the Holy Spirit changed since reading the men's stories so far?
4. How might you apply DWJWD to your own life?

Group Discussion/Share:
Address the above questions one at a time and, for those who wish to share, discuss your answers/insights.

CHAPTER 18

Twenty Years Later – All Six Men

the High School Counselor's Story

Now at a wonderful church, not far from where our original story began, the High School Counselor spent 18 years as a Youth Pastor. He recently wrote:

"As I look back over my 18 years as a Youth Pastor I have to remember some of the ups and downs which generally were as result of the general economic times, but I have been at the same church for 18 years now. No kids of my own, but I think of all the kids I've known and cared for and about, all their troubles, all their laughs and all their crises and I must pause and be grateful. I wrote a book about it.

We are warned that if something seems too good to be true it probably is. Perhaps that is why we have such a hard time grasping that God, having paid dearly for our salvation, offers it to us for free. God's gift of salvation is too good to be true but it's true. This tremendous act of generosity is what the Bible calls grace. We are saved not because of something we did or promise to do; we are saved because God, out of his kindness and mercy, purchased salvation for us and graciously offers it to us as a gift. Salvation is a free gift. We are saved by God's generosity. We are saved by his grace.

The gifts of the salvation gift package are intended by God to bring us into the fullness of life he intends for us to have and enjoy—a life of abiding love, joy, peace and goodness, a life that can only be found in God, because God himself is the source of these things. Just as life for a fish can only be found in water, the fullness of life God intends for us can only be found in a relationship with him. This is why the salvation gifts are relational in nature; they are intended to restore, renew and make possible the kind of relationship with God that God desires us to have and enjoy."

So the High School Counselor has become a noted author and seminar leader.

the Lawyer's Story

The Lawyer never forgot that pivotal "Bible Boys" conversation and is convinced it changed his life.

After taking that job at the large and well respected university, he worked there for 15 years. From there, he went on to:

- publish a 160 page coffee table book about the Holy Spirit in action *The Spirit of Fiat Lux*[5], along with a companion web site.
- re-locate the *"Run for Life*[6]*"* to the university campus

---

[5] For the story of *the Spirit of Fiat Lux*, go to www.companyofmen.net and click on "Videos".

[6] For the story of the *Run for Life*, go to www.companyofmen.net and click on "Videos".

and successfully conduct it for several years, financially benefitting local area children and youth groups. The theme remained *"Celebrating the Spirit of Goodness in Children"* with a *"Spirit Service"* immediately following the run

- incorporate the Enterprise 501c3, a non-profit educational and policy group dedicated to return public universities to focusing on the third prong of their original mission: Service to the Public[7]
- incorporate CHIERS[8] to create a Community Health Index Electronic Reporting System

When asked why he is doing all these things, his response was simple: *"Every day I try to 'Do What Jesus Would Do!'"*

While the projects are impactful, success has not been easy with any of these efforts.

- *The Spirit of Fiat Lux* coffee table book never turned into a best seller, far from it.
- The *"Run for Life"* after eight years was kicked off the campus because the football team needed the track stadium while their new football stadium was under construction.
- The Enterprise 501c3, grew to include 45 wonderful and many distinguished leaders working on higher education policy and Community Health. It may be best described by Winston Churchill's memorable slogan: *"Success is comprised of going from failure to failure without loss of enthusiasm."*
- CHIERS, comprised of a wonderfully skilled and tech-savvy staff is now just working to get over the start line as

---

[7] For the story of *Public Service Contracting*, go to www.companyofmen.net and click on "Videos".

[8] For the story of CHIERS, go to www.companyofmen.net and click on "Videos".

a cloud-based, high tech startup with a goal of *"Improving Community Health through Data Analytics."*

The key point of all these endeavors is to *"Do What Jesus Would Do!"* This does not ensure an easy path, nor a promise of success, but it remains the path, the goal, the mission.

the Pastor's Story

The Pastor relocated again, within 100 miles of the Community Church, in an agricultural region of the valley. He became Pastor to a downtown church in a town with the population of 18,000. When asked to answer the question: *"Is the Holy Spirit in your life, and if so, how?"* he responded:

> *"Your question is a good one, but I have so many projects, that I cannot give the time to answer it adequately. I'm sorry. However, there are some fine Christian websites who can address this and many other concerns better than I. Check out www.str.org, and CARM - The Christian Apologetics & Research Ministry. I have found both to be biblical and thorough. God bless you. I look forward to seeing you some time."*

the Electronics Guy's Story

The Electronics Guy and his wife are happy. They each have their own motorcycle. The Navy Veterans disability claim he put in for was finally settled in a generous way. His in-home beer-brewing and wine-making is fantastically delicious and fun. Their two daughters and three granddaughters seem to be doing great. They found a break-away small community of believers where they can be as close to God as they wish to be.

the International Banker's Story

The International Banker's story had some unbelievable twists and turns. Despite such hopeful progress, his son's eye never fully healed and the gut wrenching medical ordeal continued. His wife left him and the International Banker eventually remarried. He is still the same really great guy he always has been: kind, generous, supportive, smart, engaging, and engaged.

the Retired Salesman's Story

The Retired Salesman has since died and so has his beloved wife. Up until the end of his life, he loved God, Jesus, and the Holy Spirit, he loved his wife, his daughter, and everyone he knew. He took all that life tossed at him and said to himself every day, *"Do What Jesus Would Do!"*

Study Guide – Chapter 18:
Twenty Years Later – All Six Men

Individual Reflection:

Take 15 minutes to quietly reflect and jot down your thoughts on the following:

1. What were your thoughts/feelings about how each man turned out?
2. What lessons, if any, did you take away from each man's story?

Group Discussion/Share:

Address the above questions one at a time and, for those who wish to share, discuss your answers/insights.

CHAPTER 19

YOU TODAY

The story of the six men is finished, done, over and out. This last chapter is about you.

It comes down to four questions for you:

1. Thinking about your own unique life experiences, in the quiet of your own mind, ask yourself: *"Did I listen for the Holy Spirit during my own time of crisis?*

2. If you believe what Jesus said about the Holy Spirit, *"But I tell you the truth, it is to your advantage that I go away; for if I do not go away, the helper shall not come to you; but if I go, I will send Him to you." John 16:7,* but are not listening for the Holy Spirit ask yourself... *"Am I missing something pretty important?"*

3. Ask yourself, *"What can I start doing today to quiet myself in order to listen to the Holy Spirit?"*

4. Finally, if the Holy Spirit's message is *"Do What Jesus Would Do!"* Ask yourself... *"What am I doing today to DWJWD?"*

If nothing else, take-away one thing from this book…

DWJWD!

"Do What Jesus Would Do!"

To experience this most beautiful song, please go to our web site at www.CompanyofMen.net and move down to the song which is a YouTube video.

Enjoy and Be Inspired!

The words summarize the concepts of the book and you can enjoy and remind yourself of DWJWD. The video is a rehearsal session and we hope you treasure it as much as we do!

Performed by: TJ Burke – Director and Tenor, Janet Selby – Soprano, Marisa Barley - Alto, Jim Vandersloot – Bass

I Don't Know How to Listen

Music by Andrew Lloyd Webber/Tim Rice
New words by Brian Donohue
Supplement to *In the Company of Men*

I don't know how to listen
How to hear, how to
understand
He is God, yes really God
And He's in my heart, within
me now
How can it be?
Can it really be so simple?
Do What Jesus Would Do
They are God, yes really
God
But I've heard it all so
many times
In so many ways
Can it be so?
Can't I shut him out?
Can't I just pretend
That He isn't there?
Let my fear all out?
I never thought I'd come
to this.
Can it be so?

Don't you think it should
be easy
To forget, not to worry?
I always knew, I was so
sure
So calm, so cool, not
Satan's fool
Running all the time
This scares me so
——Music Interlude——
I never thought I'd come to
this
What's it all about?
Yet, if I learned to listen
I'd be lost, I'd be frightened
I wouldn't change, not really
change
Would I love them all?
would I serve them all?
I wouldn't want to know
This scares me so
I want this so
He loves me so

DWJWD!
Show the story – remind yourself!

See www.companyofmen.net

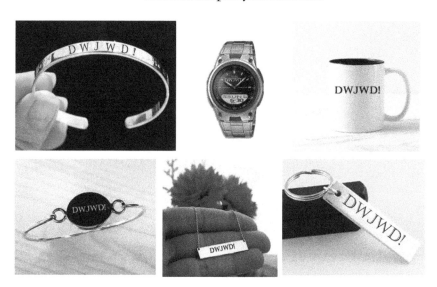

the Author

Brian Donohue and wife Dellyn have six married children and, at last counting, 15 grandchildren. Brian was a federal and state trial lawyer, worked 15 years at UC Berkeley, and is the President and Founder of the Enterprise 501c3, a California non-profit corporation. Brian authored the highly acclaimed book *The Spirit of Fiat Lux* – web site *www.SpiritofFiatLux.net*. Additionally, the Enterprise is designing and developing CHIERS - Community Health Indexing Electronics Reporting System. If you would like to learn more or become involved in any way, please contact him directly at briandonohuelaw@gmail.com

Contributor

Kathy Mendonca is an instructional designer and training specialist at University of California, Berkeley. She and her husband live in Concord, CA, and she is the proud mom of three incredible boys.